Catrin George Ponciano

111 Places Along the Algarve That You Shouldn't Miss

Dear Jaaldine, dear Mira

Wir möchten Euch neugierig machen auf mehr Portugal sehen.
Viel Freude beim Lesen wünscht die Autorin

Algarve
November
2020

emons:

Eu dedico este Livro aos meus amigos Algarvios.
I dedicate this book to all my Algarvian friends.

© Emons Verlag GmbH
All rights reserved
Photographs by Catrin George Ponciano, except:
»burros & artes« (ch. 12); Agua Mãe, Castro Marim (ch. 33);
Marion Louca (ch. 36); Anabela Gaspar (ch. 38);
João Sabino Boattours, Olhão (ch. 79); Markus Seyferth (ch. 96)
© Cover motif: shutterstock.com / MarushaBelle
Edited by Gillian Tait
Translation by Tom Ashforth
Layout: Eva Kraskes, based on a design
by Lübbeke | Naumann | Thoben
Maps: altancicek.design, www.altancicek.de
Basic cartographical information from Openstreetmap,
© OpenStreetMap-Mitwirkende, ODbL
Printing and binding: Lensing Druck GmbH & Co. KG,
Feldbachacker 16, 44149 Dortmund
Printed in Germany 2018
ISBN 978-3-7408-0381-0
First edition

Did you enjoy it? Do you want more?
Join us in uncovering new places around the world on:
www.111places.com

Foreword

Mention the Algarve, and thoughts invariably turn to the sea, to paradise beaches, red sandstone cliffs and secluded lagoon bays, to sunshine and clear blue skies, to fresh mussels and grilled fish.

The pace and rhythm of life here is quite unlike anywhere else. The whole of this coastal region seems to be under the sway of a pleasingly laid-back way of life, while each town and village has its own local flavour. The coast excels with beach coves, cliffs and lagoons, while places further inland offer a contrast, with mountains and forests. The locals welcome guests with genuine and endearing hospitality. These factors alone make the Algarve irresistible to holidaymakers and residents, to adventurers and expats. A trip through this region of Portugal is sure to be a diverse and unforgettable experience.

But the Algarve has even more to offer. Over 2,000 years of cultural history have left behind a multitude of marks and traces on its shores. In this book I follow these large, small, fantastical, magical, mystical and hidden tracks all over the region. If you want to know why the Templars' symbol of good luck was forbidden by the Inquisition, how the Black Madonna ended up in Raposeira or whether Ulysses really did visit Faro, where a family of executioners once lived or where the Portuguese mandarin is buried, what sea-bull ham or sweet potato beer taste like, then follow me through this book to 111 extraordinarily bizarre, fascinatingly mystical and uniquely exciting places on the Algarve.

Bem vindo no Algarve!

111 Places

1. Al-Buhera Sea Fort | Albufeira
   The Saracens' last barricade | 10
2. Capela da Misericórdia | Albufeira
   The lottery for beatitude | 12
3. The City Library | Albufeira
   Lídia Jorge and her message | 14
4. The Explorers Roundabout | Albufeira
   Open-air art on a traffic island | 16
5. Olhos de Água Beach | Albufeira
   Where the sea weeps | 18
6. The Skeleton Chapel | Alcantarilha
   Macabre encounter in a side chapel | 20
7. Pego Fundo | Alcoutim
   A beach without the sea | 22
8. Executioners' Village | Aldeia do Carrasco
   The exorcists of the Inquisition | 24
9. The Country Bakery | Alferce
   Antoíneta and her mother yeast | 26
10. Berenike's Library | Aljezur
    Meeting place for bookworms from around the world | 28
11. Cemitério de Aljezur | Aljezur
    NATO comes to visit | 30
12. The Donkey Farm | Aljezur
    Sofia has a soft spot for jennies and jacks | 32
13. The Hill of the Beheaded | Aljezur
    When the elders hold court | 34
14. The Gold-Grass Village | Alte
    Delicate craftwork in golden straw | 36
15. The Margarida Chapel | Alte
    The brave peasant girl and the dragon | 38
16. The Bar at the Penina Hotel | Alvor
    A peace treaty that instigated a war | 40
17. Lota Fish Hall | Alvor
    It's all about the fish | 42
18. The Rossio Relief | Alvor
    King Dom João II and Portugal's armillary sphere | 44

19	Ameixial Services	Ameixial
	Doll's house atmosphere at the end of the Algarve	46

20   The Casino With No Future | Armação de Pêra
Art, kitsch and curiosities | 48

21   The Needle Rock | Arrifana
A guide and protector | 50

22   Ponta da Atalaia | Arrifana
The chosen place of legendary Sufi knights | 52

23   The Cockerel Stone | Barão de São João
Cock-a-doodle-doo from the Stone Age | 54

24   The Ara Vitae Sculpture | Benafim
Borges' search for the cradle of humanity | 56

25   The Bensafrim Stone | Bensafrim
An upside-down message | 58

26   The New Village School | Boliqueime
Petrol station owner's son becomes president | 60

27   The Accordion Capital | Bordeira
The soul of folk music is in Bordeira | 62

28   The Os Agostos Estate | Bordeira
Chamber music with nibbles in the barn | 64

29   The Factory Beach | Cacela Velha
A touch of the South Seas on the Algarve | 66

30   The Land and Sea Museum | Carrapateira
Where the farmers are fishermen too | 68

31   The DEKA Community Centre | Carvoeiro
Ecumenical services with the sound of the sea | 70

32   The Salt Spa | Castro Marim
Bathing in sea salt for well-being | 72

33   The Symbol of the Castle | Castro Marim
A medieval knight welcomes you | 74

34   The Beach Fortress | Conceição de Tavira
An extra guard for the tuna | 76

35   The Grotto of Venus | Estoi
Three delightful nymphs and their Zeus | 78

36   The Escape Route | Estômbar
Race for justice on a three-wheeler | 80

37   The Grotto of the Vizier | Estômbar
Secret tunnel of caliphs and kings | 82

38   The Spring-water Park | Estômbar
Splashy fun in summer or winter | 84

39	The Grain Barn | Faro	
	The Greek riddle of Faro | 86	
40	The Jewish Cemetery | Faro	
	Portugal's first printed book | 88	
41	The Obelisk of Faro | Faro	
	Portugal's most famous slap in the face | 90	
42	The Old Harbour Inn | Faro	
	Senhor Joaquim and his cherubs | 92	
43	The Old Power Station | Faro	
	Experience the sea with all your senses | 94	
44	The Slaughterhouse by the Park | Faro	
	Paradise for peacocks and strollers | 96	
45	The Mandarin's Grave | Ferragudo	
	The final resting place of a restless man | 98	
46	The Scout Memorial | Ferragudo	
	Scouts take their pledge by the anchor | 100	
47	The Spirulina Algae Farm | Fóia	
	Spirulina pioneers on the summit | 102	
48	The Petanca Court | Fuseta	
	Sporadic rendezvous for a game of pétanque | 104	
49	The River Fishing Museum | Guerreiros do Rio	
	Village of river warriors and smugglers | 106	
50	The Fado Bar | Lagoa	
	A young girl on the path to becoming a fado diva | 108	
51	The Quinta dos Vales Vineyard | Lagoa	
	Where the customers create their own cuvées | 110	
52	The Red Boulevard | Lagoa	
	Strolling along silent asphalt | 112	
53	The São José Convent | Lagoa	
	The secret of Ó | 114	
54	The Chapel of St Anthony | Lagos	
	José Saramago and the people | 116	
55	The Church of Santa Maria | Lagos	
	Here lies Henry the Navigator | 118	
56	The Havaneza Café | Lagos	
	Meeting place for Masonic conspiracy | 120	
57	The Putting Garden | Lagos	
	Playing mini-golf on the roof | 122	
58	The Riverside Car Park | Lagos	
	The harbour foundation stone is in the basement | 124	

59	The Terminus | Lagos	
	Slowing right down by train | 126	
60	The da Graça Monastery | Loulé	
	No admission for demons | 128	
61	The Lieutenant's Square | Loulé	
	Mistake of a revolutionary | 130	
62	The Piedade Hill | Loulé	
	Puffing and panting for the matriarch | 132	
63	The Poets' Café | Loulé	
	People's poet António Aleixo and his quatrains | 134	
64	The Buddhist Stupa | Malhão	
	A sacred place on the Serra do Mú | 136	
65	The Santinha | Marmelete	
	A village learns to learn | 138	
66	The Tollhouse-Madhouse | Mexilhoeira de Carregação	
	The king's extra-extra fig tax | 140	
67	Algarve Motorsports Park | Mexilhoeira Grande	
	Motorsport fun to watch and join in with | 142	
68	The Parish Church | Mexilhoeira Grande	
	A generous count and his fear of purgatory | 144	
69	Cerro da Cabeça | Moncarapacho	
	A hike on the trail of Atlantis | 146	
70	The Catarina College | Monchique	
	A holistic modern school for girls | 148	
71	The Fire Station | Monchique	
	Mountain village on the alert | 150	
72	The Medronho Boutique | Monchique	
	The firewater of Monchique | 152	
73	Salvador's Workshop | Monchique	
	Every wooden puzzle becomes a folding chair | 154	
74	The Lawn Bowls Club | Montes de Alvor	
	Bowling without skittles or pins | 156	
75	The Skydiving Centre | Montes de Alvor	
	Meeting place for sky surfers | 158	
76	The Beach Paradise | Odeceixe	
	Sunbathing on one of Portugal's natural wonders | 160	
77	Fonte Santa | Odelouca	
	Only a few know the way to the holy spring | 162	
78	The João Lúcio Palace | Olhão	
	The sad poet and his fairytale castle | 164	

| 79 | The Ria Formosa Nature Reserve | Olhão
A seaweed meadow for seahorses | 166
| 80 | Santa Maria Lighthouse | Olhão
222 steps to the best view of the coast | 168
| 81 | The Tidal Mill | Olhão
Bela Moura Floripes and her admirers | 170
| 82 | The Museum of *A Avezinha* | Paderne
The four Marias and their newspaper | 172
| 83 | The Feather Cliffs | Penina
Picturesque trail in the Serra de Caldeirão | 174
| 84 | The Algarve Potteries | Porches
Insider meeting place for music fans and expats | 176
| 85 | The House of Fear | Portimão
The long shadow of the secret police | 178
| 86 | The Junction of Freedom | Portimão
Three streets tell the story of revolution | 180
| 87 | The President's Office | Portimão
Where the spirit of the city's father walks | 182
| 88 | Quinta do Marisco | Portimão
Scrabbling lobsters and lively lugworms | 184
| 89 | The Sardine Cannery | Portimão
Tinned fish and its epicurean comeback | 186
| 90 | The Stone Tear | Portimão
The Stone Age rock in the middle of the pavement | 188
| 91 | The University Cellar | Portimão
Mystical water reservoir from the Arabian Nights | 190
| 92 | The Soares Residence | Praia de Alemão in Vau
Private refuge of the founding father of democracy | 192
| 93 | The Olhão Argonauts | Quelfes
David against Goliath | 194
| 94 | The Museum of Water | Querença
The Portuguese donkey and the Arabian well | 196
| 95 | The Guadalupe Chapel | Raposeira
The Black Madonna of Raposeira | 198
| 96 | The Sweet Potato Restaurant | Rogil
A potato with a place in every cooking pot | 200
| 97 | The Electric Tuk-Tuk | Sagres
Cruising the Cape of Sagres with zero horsepower | 202
| 98 | The Pet Cemetery | Sagres
The final resting place for dogs and cats | 204

99	The Archaeological Trail	São Bartolomeu de Messines
	Past red standing stones into the present	206
100	The Cork Factory	São Brás de Alportel
	How the cork gets from the tree into the bottle	208
101	The Library Cellar	Silves
	Roman waste management	210
102	The Cross of Portugal	Silves
	Manueline masterpiece with history	212
103	The New City Hall	Silves
	A reckless three-way liaison	214
104	The House of Álvaro de Campos	Tavira
	The author that never existed	216
105	Quatro Aguas	Tavira
	Where four waterways meet	218
106	The Tuna Fish Museum	Tavira
	The bull of the sea	220
107	The Railway Station	Tunes
	A rebellious bank robber and his greatest coup	222
108	Praia do Castelejo	Vila do Bispo
	An informer's last step	224
109	Cabanas Square	Vila Nova de Cacela
	A revolutionary discovers art as a haven of peace	226
110	The Dune Sanctuary	Vila Real de Santo António
	Encountering chameleons in the wild	228
111	The Ferry to Portugal	Vila Real de Santo António
	The end of the journey is the start of the journey	230

ALBUFEIRA

1 Al-Buhera Sea Fort
The Saracens' last barricade

You can reach the beach in Albufeira by taking the lift, stairs or escalator, or by walking right through the cliffs via a tunnel. The modern city, which boasts a starfish as its symbol, stands on a group of hills, and the old town is built right up to the edge of the sandstone cliffs of the coast. The fishermen's quarter nestles up to the Praia dos Pescadores beach, and an area peppered with nightclubs and restaurants spreads out all the way to Avenida da Liberdade.

The 'unassailable' Moorish sea fort of Al-Buhera once sat atop the cliffs over the Praia do Peneco beach. Steps next to the beach tunnel lead to the cliff top. From there you walk left, past the clock tower, to the old market place at the main gate of the former fortress. The oval whitewashed concrete rampart in the centre of the square is a miniature, stylised imitation of the battlements of the inner wall of the double-fortified sea fort. This is where the remaining soldiers of the last emirs of Al-Gharb held out, barricaded in behind high walls, defending the fortress to the last man against the advancing Crusaders of the conquistador king Dom Afonso III.

The exposed wall foundations and two cisterns visible in the archaeological excavation site are about 1,000 years old; these are the only traces left on the cliffs of the legendary Al-Buhera fortress. The inner ramparts of the frequently contested fort were completely destroyed. There are still some fragments of the outer fortifications that once encompassed the entire hill, visible on street corners at the end of narrow, shaded passageways in the former castle district. The houses here are so close together that you can only get around on foot. Arcade arches mark the sites of ancient city gates. All is calm here in the alleyways of the former sea fort, just a few steps away from the beating heart of the biggest tourist metropolis on the Algarve.

Address Museu de Arqueológia de Albufeira, Praça da República 1, 8200 Albufeira | Getting there A 22, exit 9, IC 1/N 395 Albufeira, left at the Explorers Roundabout, right at the lights, park on the way to the city centre, walk towards the tunnel to the beach, go up the stairs at the tourist office, then left past the clock tower to the museum | Hours Tue–Sun 9.30am–5.30pm, with a midday break | Tip If you turn right at the top of the stairs you will find Albufeira's three main churches as well as the Museum of Sacred Art.

ALBUFEIRA

2 Capela da Misericórdia
The lottery for beatitude

On a side street only a few metres away from the cliffs, a wooden door in a plain portal with a pointed arch closes this chapel off from the world. The house of god has been abandoned, and currently serves the local parish as a store for religious props. It is rarely open, which is a great shame, as the chapel has many stories to tell.

After the Christian reconquest, the former Muslim mihrab was turned over to a new purpose, as a private chapel for the future castellans of Albufeira. The Islamic prayer niche was replaced by a Catholic altar, and the church was reconsecrated. Three centuries later, Eleanor of Lancaster created the charitable ecclesiastical order of Santa Casa de Misericórdia. The castellan of Albufeira of the time supported the queen and her newly founded charity for the needy by gifting her the chapel and all its outbuildings. It has survived to this day as the very first such charity on the Algarve. As an expression of her gratitude for the generous donation, Eleanor granted the castellan and his wife a final resting place in a crypt under the altar. The Santa Casa charity grew rapidly, and branches cropped up all over the country. But the number of people in need grew as well, and soon collections alone weren't sufficient to finance the royal charity. In search of additional sources of income for the offertory box, the charity devised the idea of a game of chance, the holy Santa Casa lottery.

Since then the coffers have always been full. Tickets can be bought on the street from news kiosks, or from members of staff of the Santa Casa organisation. The lottery for beatitude has continued to grow, and today the holy Santa Casa lottery system includes the EuroMillions draw and the Totoloto lottery. The draws take place weekly, and the charity uses the profit to maintain its churches, nursing homes and kindergartens.

Address Capelinha da Misericórdia, Rua Henrique Calado 5–9, 8200 Albufeira | **Getting there** A 22, exit 9, IC 1/N 395 Albufeira, left at the Explorers Roundabout, right at the traffic lights, park on Avenida da Liberdade, go up the stairs at the tourist office, then left and left again at the Archaeological Museum | **Tip** Tapete Mágico, a 10-minute walk away on Rua Oceano, is the in-house shop at Santa Casa da Misericórdia's main building. It sells hand-woven wool carpets with traditional Algarve patterns, the like of which you're unlikely to find elsewhere (Mon–Fri, mornings).

3 The City Library
Lídia Jorge and her message

The city library of Albufeira is called Biblioteca Municipal Lídia Jorge – a choice of name that is a homage to the world-renowned author from the Algarve. The Portuguese writer of novels, which have been translated into over 30 languages around the world, was born in 1946, and studied Romance philology at the University of Lisbon. In 1970 she accompanied her then husband, who served as a soldier in the colonial wars, to Africa, and lived with him for many years in Angola and Mozambique, where she worked as a teacher. Her profound encounters with African culture, steeped in the climate of war, inspired Lídia Jorge to work through her observations in written form after returning to Portugal. Her debut *The Day of the Prodigies* was published a few years after the 1974 Carnation Revolution, and was one of the first books in Portugal to deal with the Portuguese colonial wars in Africa in novel form. One of her later novels, *The Murmuring Coast*, was made into a film in 2004. It tells the story, in the guise of a flashback, of a young woman who arrives in Mozambique as the wife of a soldier and becomes entangled in the chaos of war. The impact of war on people and their relationships was the predominant theme in many of the author's stories, before she discovered the Algarve as a new backdrop for her novels.

Having received several international prizes for literature, and been appointed *Commandeur de l'Ordre des Arts et des Lettres* in France, Lídia Jorge now writes novels about her Portuguese homeland. Her characters are notable for their insubordinate nature and other clearly defined traits of genuine Algarvians. She is a role model for other female authors. Her courage in writing experimentally has encouraged women in particular to take a career as an author seriously. In Albufeira, Lídia Jorge is seen as an ambassador for local culture, traditions and language.

Address Biblioteca Municipal Lídia Jorge, Rua Sophia de Mello Breyner 46, 8200 Albufeira | Getting there A 22, exit 9, IC 1 / N 395 Albufeira, left at the Explorers Roundabout, left at the roundabout with the colourful pipes, right at the next roundabout | Hours Mon – Fri 9.30am – 7pm | Tip The library holds an archive of the local newspaper *A Avezinha*, a comprehensive eyewitness to three consecutive epochs: republic, dictatorship, republic. The former offices of the paper, which incorporate a museum, are 15 kilometres away in Paderne.

ALBUFEIRA

4_ The Explorers Roundabout
Open-air art on a traffic island

The 16 districts of the Algarve all show off their prowess in the design of their roundabouts, outdoing one another either with botanical and artistic extravagance, or by leaving them bare and renting them out for advertising. For this reason, no two roundabouts are the same. Gardeners, artists and advertising experts lend each roundabout an individual face, embellishing the cityscape with artistic creations. Despite stiff competition, the most beautiful of these are to be found in Albufeira – this city is the uncrowned queen of Algarve roundabouts.

The Rotundas de Albufeira guide traffic from the marina in the west right through the city to Santa Eulália in the east, and they also serve as orientation points for drivers. In Albufeira no one sends an unfamiliar driver straight on, right or left through the city – that would end in chaos, or in some dead end in the old town. Here you are guided to your destination by way of the roundabouts. From the Clock Roundabout you reach the shopping centre, and to get to the regional hospital you go past the colourful, intertwined pipes that look like worms. The road to Olhos de Água forks off at the armillary sphere, while the leaping marble dolphins point the way to the historic part of town.

As soon as the sun begins to set, the roundabouts are lit up in iridescent light. Though the *rotundas* are attractions during the day, they become really romantic when illuminated in the dark. The most impressive installation in this roadway gallery is the Explorers Roundabout. Here drivers on the motorway slip road are greeted by a caravel sailing ship attached to a 10-metre-high steel-brace sail, with the cross of the Order of Christ mounted in the middle. At dusk the sail shines brightly, illuminated by thousands of little lamps, the water fountains sparkle in blue, the sail in white and the cross in vermilion.

Address Rotunda dos Descobrimentos, Avenida dos Descobrimentos, 8200 Albufeira | **Getting there** A 22, exit 9, IC 27/ N 395 Albufeira leads straight to the Explorers Roundabout | **Tip** Albufeira marina is just a few minutes' drive and two roundabouts west of the Explorers Roundabout. There are many maritime activities you can take part in, from diving to dolphin tours.

ALBUFEIRA

5 Olhos de Água Beach
Where the sea weeps

To the east of Albufeira is Olhos de Água, a small fishing port and beach. A dozen wooden huts painted light blue stand at the edge of the beach; fishermen sit in front of them repairing their nets. Their boats lie keel-up on a concrete ramp far from the water. On the narrow promenade date palms grow, and a handful of cafés offer refreshments, along with a magnificent view of the bay. At first glance this just seems to be yet another example of a beautiful beach on Albufeira's ochre-red Falesia sandstone coast, of the kind that adorns every holiday brochure about the Algarve. But twice a day the left side of the bay is transformed into something quite extraordinary. As the sea goes out, the so-called Olheiras de Água emerge from the water, among the seaweed-covered rocks of the reef.

Water bubbles up out of the sand at the sea end of the rocks – it looks almost as though the sea itself has eyes that are streaming with tears. That is why the beach is called Olhos de Água – 'eyes of the sea'. But strangely enough this water is fresh, not saline. Fresh water springs in the sea, like this one, are a real natural phenomenon, but are very rare. An old fishermen's legend tells of a pretty young woman, who first lost her beloved, and then shortly afterwards her own life, to the tide. The pearls of fresh water are her tears, so the story goes, as this is where the sad young woman lies, buried deep beneath the sand.

The TV soap *Olhos de Àgua* – the most successful series ever on Portuguese television – has a theme tune that reflects this melancholy, based on a melody passed down by fishermen. As sung by the cult Portuguese singer António Ferrão, better know as Toy, the song has become a favourite among lovers, as well as those mourning lost love. Stairs lead down to the beach and rocks of Olhos de Água, but it is only at low tide that the sea weeps.

Address Praia dos Olhos de Água, Rua dos Pescadores 3, 8200 Albufeira | **Getting there** A 22, exit 9, IC 1/ N 395 Albufeira, left at the Explorers Roundabout towards the east, follow signs to Santa Eulália and Olhos de Água | **Tip** You can reach Albufeira's famous ochre-red sandstone Falesia beach by foot along a cliff-top trail, while the hippest nightclub in the Algarve, Le Club, is five minutes' drive away on Santa Eulália beach.

ALCANTARILHA

6 The Skeleton Chapel
Macabre encounter in a side chapel

Alcantarilha is located between Albufeira and Lagoa. The village itself is neither particularly important nor especially well known. Its most famous features are perhaps its bridges. There is the old bridge, over which seafarers, Saracens and Crusaders once rode from Faro towards the west, if they wanted to avoid a detour of several kilometres to cross the Ribeira de Alcantarilha gorge. And there's the new bridge, which everyone drives over nowadays to reach the motorway in the direction of Lagoa and Silves, or Faro and Lisbon.

The village of bridges sits on a hill, the church steeple towers over the colourfully tiled rooftops and indicates the way to the centre. Here, just like in the old days, everyday life still plays out around the church. There's a mini supermarket that sells everything from toothpaste to incontinence pads. The square boasts a cash machine, post office, local government office, fire station and of course the church, where services and the occasional concert take place.

It isn't the church itself that we're interested in, though, but an adjoining chapel in its rear corner to the right, which is accessed from the outside of the building. A small sign reading *Capela dos Ossos* points the way to this extremely unusual attraction. Take a deep breath, count to 10 and prepare yourself emotionally before going in, as you are about to enter a crypt of death. The walls, ceiling and altar of the chapel are all lined with the skulls, bones and vertebrae of around 1,500 skeletons from the former cemetery of Alcantarilha. When the old cemetery was declared a construction development site, the skeletons were dug up and given a collective final resting place. 'Where we rest, we wait for you' is their message. It is an oppressively silent place, in an eerily precise Baroque style, on the threshold between this world and the next.

Address Capela dos Ossos, Largo do Ossário, 8365 Alcantarilha | Getting there A 22, exit 7, N 125 Alcantarilha, exit towards Centro/Igréja on the roundabout at the far side of the village; park at the church and follow the sign to Capela dos Ossos | Tip Five minutes' drive along the N 125 from Alcantarilha towards Faro, then on the M 524 in the direction of Algoz, is the biggest sand sculpture park in Europe, FIESA.

ALCOUTIM

7 — Pego Fundo
A beach without the sea

The market town of Alcoutim climbs up the side of the hill on the Portuguese bank of the Guadiana River, opposite the Spanish fort of San Marcos de Sanlucár. Here, depending on the tide, the riverbank can tower several metres above the water, and most of the time the Rio Guadiana flows gently by, though the actual strength of the currents is occasionally betrayed by spiralling vortices on the water surface. The speed of the river's flow varies, and is affected by the ebb and flow of the ocean, 30 kilometres away – its direction can change in the blink of an eye, determined by the tide and its pull. The Guadiana's currents are treacherous. Although it seems to glide sedately by Alcoutim, swimming in the river is definitely not recommended, and even paddling in a canoe or kayak is inadvisable unless you are highly experienced.

In Alcoutim the sun shines for weeks on end during the summer, and the air vibrates with heat as temperatures rise to over 40 degrees Celsius. Everyone craves a place to cool off, but the sea and its beaches are an hour's drive away. Acquatic refreshment can only be found in private swimming pools, under the garden hose or, since recently, at the Praia Fluvial do Pego Fundo municipal beach. This artificial beach – not the only one of its kind in Portugal – was created by dumping tons of sand in a valley on the banks of the small Ribeira de Cadavais river. With its park areas and sand banks, it offers a deceptively good alternative to the fun of a beach by the sea.

Admittedly the sound of the waves is missing, but the gentle rustle of the reeds is just as relaxing. Alcoutim beach is designed to be accessible to disabled users, and it is family friendly, equipped with a snack bar, toilets, playground and car park. It has now grown into a popular leisure attraction, for bathing in the summer and also for staging cultural events.

Address Praia Fluvial do Pego Fundo, 8970 Alcoutim | Getting there A 22, exit 18, IC 27 towards Beja, turn right on to the N 124 at Balurcos, further on the N 122-1 to Alcoutim, follow the signs to Praia Fluvial do Pego Fundo | Tip The market town of Alcoutim offers the chance to witness the ancient handicrafts of basket making and wool weaving. On the quayside you can also book a boat trip upriver to Mértola in Alentejo.

8 Executioners' Village
The exorcists of the Inquisition

Sheep graze peacefully, vines grow, and young families pursue their dream lives of owning their own house with a back garden. But what is now the quiet Portimão suburb of Aldeia do Carrasco was once home to a family of executioners who served the infamous Inquisition. That is why it's known as the Village of Executioners, even though the family line has long since died out, and execution has been a thing of the past in Portugal since 1856.

Most of the victims of these hooded men were not even criminals, but rather targets of the Inquisition. Although witch hunting wasn't quite as extensive in medieval Portugal as it was in the north of Europe, the methods of 'exorcism' used to lead those condemned as heretics back to the so-called right path were sadistic, vicious and perverse, and most of the accused didn't survive the ordeal.

The Inquisition reached absolute boiling point at Easter in 1506 with the Lisbon Massacre, when, in the course of a single weekend, the king, Dom Manuel I, had a total of 4,000 Jews first tortured, then executed and burned on Rossio Square in Lisbon. Under the subsequent rule of his son, a particularly vicious secret society, led by the king's younger brother Cardinal Dom Henrique, was formed in Monsaraz. Their hired executioners were nearly all members of the same family, from the village of Aldeia do Carrasco. They were particular specialists in torture methods involving fire and water. The executioner brothers from the Algarve knew many ways to inflict pain, and they earned a decent bounty for each assignment. After the near-execution of a folk hero was revoked at the very last second, with the poor man's head already on the chopping block, the tide finally turned. The profession of executioner died out, and with it the family of exorcists from Portimão. Today the Chico Maria pub stands on the site of their house.

Address Rua das Flores 31, 8500 Portimão, Aldeia do Carrasco | **Getting there** A 22, exit 4 towards Alvor, turn left towards Portimão after the second roundabout, follow the main road for about two kilometres, until a sign on the left points the way to the restaurant Chico Maria | **Tip** Around eight kilometres' drive in the direction of Lagos, on the right in the direction of Monchique, are the Stone Age excavations of Alcalar. On the way there you'll pass the Quinta do Morgado da Torre vineyard, where you can buy exquisite red wine made with old grape varieties, or take part in wine tastings and guided tours through the cellars.

ALFERCE

9 The Country Bakery
Antoíneta and her mother yeast

Monchique marks the beginning of another world. Nature rules here, and everything in life is bound up with it. The mountain chain is densely forested, and hollowed out by a multitude of underground water reservoirs. Once you turn off the first roundabout in Monchique towards Alferce, you leave the tourist face of the Algarve behind and are headed straight into the wilderness. The road leads past firewood sellers, potato farmers, a sausage factory and down-to-earth pubs. On the left-hand side, after five kilometres, you will reach a relic of ancient tavern culture, the Malhada Quente. Just before the tavern, a steep road forks to the left into a valley, leading you to a tiny hamlet.

From early in the morning, be it summer or winter, there is always smoke drifting from the chimney on the roof of the first house. Here the bread is still baked the old-fashioned way, in a wood-fired oven. You will smell the unmistakable aroma of Pão Caseiro as soon as you step out of your car. The pillowy wheat bread, with its crispy, knobbly crust, is part of every Algarvian meal. Plenty of cistus bush brushwood is needed to fire up the oven, and a decent mother yeast or 'starter' is required to make it. Master baker Antoíneta was given her mother yeast by a fellow baker in Alentejo. She has looked after it for more than five years, here in her bakery Pão Branco Quente, beating, kneading and airing it every day so that it rises and grows again and again.

'Those I break bread with – they are my friends,' she says, fetching a freshly baked loaf from the oven, breaking it into pieces, pouring olive oil into a bowl and inviting her guests to share *tiborna*, bread in olive oil. Together with Antoíneta's devotion to bread baking, the warm feeling evoked by the frugal meal is sure to create a real sense of home, and make you want to come back again very soon.

Address Pão Branco Quente, Malhada Quente, 8550 Monchique-Alferce | **Getting there** A 22, exit 6, towards Monchique, at the entrance to the village turn right towards Alferce, after five kilometres the access road turns off to the left in front of the Malhada Quente tavern and leads directly to the bakery | **Tip** The Picota, a mountain between Alferce and Monchique, can be explored by car on country roads, or by hiking the circular trail PR 2 MCQ.

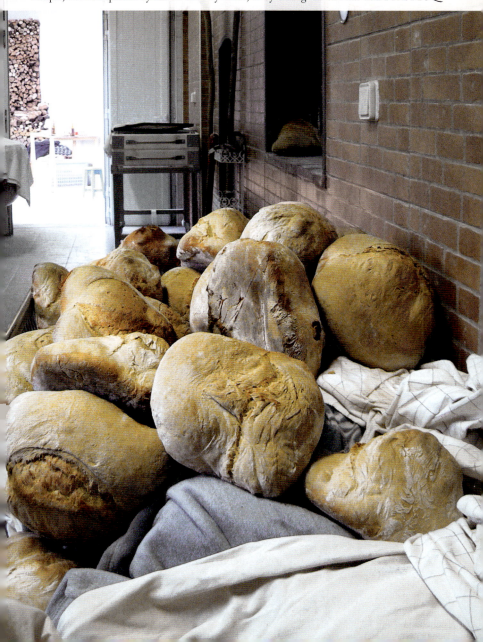

ALJEZUR

10 Berenike's Library
Meeting place for bookworms from around the world

This lending library, a private initiative of the German expatriate Berenike Jacob, has been a fixture of Aljezur's cultural landscape since it was founded nearly six years ago. The private library is housed in what was formerly a local council coach garage. Here Berenike has compiled a considerable selection of more than 4,000 German-language books, as well as over 1,000 Portuguese titles. The lion's share of her collection are whodunits, thrillers and novels. According to Berenike, whodunits are the most popular read, particularly among holidaymakers. She is always looking out for new books to freshen up the existing offer. So you'll generally find current titles from the German-language book world, as well as lots of popular novels, in Berenike's library.

Berenike's library has over 100 members. Bookworms come regularly from Aljezur and the surrounding region for a supply of new reading material, or to use the library to work and surf the internet. Berenike's library has long been well known among bibliophiles from the German-speaking diaspora in the area between São Teotónio in Alentejo, Monchique in the mountains and Lagos by the sea. There are posters in the library windows advertising the wide range of events currently taking place in the region. These could be music festivals, yoga by the sea or choir groups, cycling, rubbish clear-ups or surfing championships.

The county of Aljezur, in the far north-west of the Algarve, is home to the largest resident community of German immigrants in the south of Portugal, many of whom meet up in the library, some regularly, others only sporadically. 'It's a meeting place of books, people and languages,' Berenike says, smiling contentedly. Book reviews, talks, film nights and much more take place at the Biblioteca Aljezur, in collaboration with the local cultural association Tertúlia.

Address Rua de Lisboa 10, 8670 Aljezur, www.bibliotecaaljezur.com | **Getting there** A 22 to Bensafrim, towards Aljezur, turn left before the bridge, follow the road uphill to the junction, Rua de Lisboa is on the right | **Hours** Mon & Thu 11am–5pm | **Tip** On the roof of the library is Aljezur's former place of execution. Two marble sculptures there commemorate Henry the Navigator and the beginning of the Age of Discovery, 600 years ago.

11 Cemitério de Aljezur
NATO comes to visit

The entrance to the cemetery on the crest of the hill in the Aljezur district of Igréja Nova doesn't look particularly inviting – two skulls with crossbones, in the style of a Jolly Roger, await visitors at the gate. Here, wealthy families have built private mausoleums as their final resting places and had them decorated with imaginative ornamentation and images of heavenly creatures. Individual graves are spread out around the family crypts. These low-lying graves are decorated with plastic or nylon flowers and memorial plaques, and are framed with white marble plates.

Close to the centre of the cemetery are seven graves that really stand out against the otherwise rather run-of-the-mill graveyard scene. Engraved on each of the dark granite headstones is the *Balkenkreuz* of the German air defence from World War II. Seven German names and the respective ranks of the deceased are written underneath. Their collective date of death is given as 9 July, 1943. It was on this day that a British RAF fighter plane on patrol surprised a German Luftwaffe bomber with a crew of seven on board as it flew along the coast of Aljezur, eventually bringing it down after a tenacious dogfight over Arrifana beach. The aircraft crashed into a cliff, and the whole crew were killed immediately.

Locals recovered the dead from the wreckage and buried them in the cemetery in Aljezur. A few years ago members of the German Protestant parish in Carvoeiro held the first ever memorial service specifically organised for the seven men of the Luftwaffe in Aljezur. Since then it has become a tradition that every year on Remembrance Day a memorial service takes place at the graves of the airmen. This is followed by a minute's silence and a wreath-laying ceremony, with representatives of the Catholic Church in Aljezur, and delegates from NATO and the German Foreign Office in Lisbon.

Address Cemitério Municipal de Aljezur, Rua do Cemitério, 8670 Aljezur | **Getting there** A 22 to Bensafrim, N 120 Aljezur, towards Lisbon at the roundabout, turn right at the fire station, right again at the end of the road, then the first road on the left leads to the cemetery | **Tip** The site of the crash in Arrifana is 15 minutes' drive away: head back towards Lagos on the N 120 and turn right just after the sign for Aljezur on to the country road M 1003 to Arrifana. The fishing village in the cliffs is well known for its surfing beach.

ALJEZUR

12 The Donkey Farm
Sofia has a soft spot for jennies and jacks

If you want to experience the Algarve in a completely different and untroubled way, take a walk on the right track with a donkey as your companion. The German Sofia von Mentzingen picked up the idea of using donkeys as trekking buddies in France, and she has now granted the cuddly long-eared creatures a future on the Algarve, with a variety of new initiatives. Once again you'll find the humble donkey carrying out duties old and new, as pack animals and hiking companions, as well as helping in therapy and coaching. Sofia set up Burros & Artes in 2009 along with the artist Elsa Ribeiro, offering the first donkey tours on the Algarve, together with workshops in traditional handicrafts.

This was a brave step for the newly fledged proprietor of the one-woman business – alongside the daily duties of taking care of the growing herd of donkeys, there is also the marketing and scheduling of tours, and supervision of guests to see to. Donkeys never rest, but when a new donkey joins the group, it can take up to two years, depending on its background and age, before it is able to carry out its duties reliably. But if you take good care of these animals, feed them, provide for them and give them space and time, they will reward you richly with their trust and willingness, and touch you with their gentleness. You travel light on a donkey hike, as they can carry up to 30 kilos of luggage and children. In return, you will adapt to their pace, not the other way round.

Whether on a guided tour or an individual trek, the donkey walks are based on routes through west Algarve and the Monchique mountains. Treks vary in length from several days, with overnight stops, on the long-distance Via Algarviana and Rota Vicentina walking routes, to half- or full-day tours around the donkey yard, through the old town of Aljezur or to the wonderful dune beach of Amoreira.

Address Burros & Artes, Vale das Amoreiras, 8670 Aljezur, www.donkey-trekking-algarve.blogspot.com | **Getting there** A 22 to Bensafrim, towards Aljezur, left at the only roundabout, right towards Carrascalinho at the fire station (Bombeiros), continue 2.5 kilometres out of town to the turn-off, following the signs for Vale das Amoreiras | **Tip** On the way back to Aljezur from the donkey farm you will come to the newer part of the town. The Igreja Matriz de Nossa Senhora da Alva church and Galeria Espaço + are both worth a visit, as are the market hall with its fresh regional produce and the charming café-pub down by the river.

ALJEZUR

13 — The Hill of the Beheaded
When the elders hold court

The market town of Aljezur stretches over three hills. The former Moorish stronghold of Castelo de Aljezur stands defiant on the crest of the middle hill. The old town spreads down the slope beneath it, terrace by terrace, towards the riverbank. Aljezur was the only port town between Sagres and Lisbon, and thus an important market place – the river was navigable, and the harbour right below the castle. The market, a centre of trade for seafarers, was roughly in the middle, in front of what are now the local history museum and car park.

Merchants from all around the world, along with the crooks and thieves that inevitably accompanied them, came to Aljezur. However both the Saracens, and after them the castellans of Aljezur, made very short shrift of thieves. Villains were accused, sentenced and beheaded at one fell swoop. Heads would roll all the way down to the old market place, where they were displayed atop spikes, just as in Djemaa el Fna square in Marrakesh, as a deterrent to misdemeanour. The court was held on a plateau on the lower hill next to the castle hill. The market has now moved to the hall by the river, and the court has long since closed.

Nowadays, however, the plateau on the crown of the hill serves as a daily meeting place for the older generation from the surrounding neighbourhood, who exchange the most recent gossip and 'Did you hear about so-and-so?', passing judgement on their neighbours under a pledge of secrecy. This is why young people jokingly call the hill the *tribunal* – high court. The place is a fantastic vantage point, as well as the starting point for a long walk over Aljezur's three hills, to the castle, right through the old town to the museum and to the river, further along the banks to the memorial to the rice women, over the river on the antique bridge, and back uphill through the other side of the old town.

Address Travessa do Forte 1, 8670 Aljezur | **Getting there** A 22 to Bensafrim, continue towards Aljezur, turn left before the bridge in Aljezur, follow the road to the church, park there, walk along Rua da Forte to the viewing platform on your right | **Tip** The walking route through historic Aljezur and the surrounding area is six kilometres long in total and begins and ends at the pedestrian bridge on the river. The route will take you to all of the sights and takes around two hours.

ALTE

14 — The Gold-Grass Village
Delicate craftwork in golden straw

The mountain village of Alte is in Barrocal, in the middle of the Serra de Caldeirão. The name is derived from *barro*, meaning 'clay', and *cal*, meaning 'chalk'. Almond, fig and carob trees feel at home here – they like the dry climate, the barren earth and the constant wind blowing in from the sea. As in every other village in the Algarve hinterland, everyday life here revolves around the parish church. The alleyways away from the church are tranquil – the young work on the coast or abroad, and most of Alte's inhabitants are over 60. This wasn't always the case. In the past, all the villagers worked, and especially the women – in fact Alte was known as the village of hardworking women.

During the day they toiled in the fields, and in the evenings they would be on the threshing floor. In the spring they moved to work in the rice fields of Setúbal, in the summer they returned and harvested fruit at home in Alte. Their pay was extremely meagre, just enough to buy essentials, sometimes not even that. They earned a little extra with craftwork made of the golden grass called esparto. The long, thin, shiny golden blades that grow thick and tall around the many springs near Alte are ideal for weaving, after laborious preparation.

After finishing work in the fields, the peasant women would set off again in the evening to cut the golden esparto, tying the straws into bundles and carrying them back to the communal threshing floor in the village. First they soaked the grass in water, then they crushed the blades into fine strips, which they later wove into pretty baskets and bags. A tiled panel on Rua dos Pisadoiros shows the busy women and their ancient handicraft. Nowadays you can still find craftwork made of esparto at street markets, but these golden-straw trinkets are made by hardworking Brazilian women, and no longer by the *pisadoiros* from Alte.

Address Rua dos Pisadoiros, 8100 Alte | **Getting there** Motorway junction Albufeira, A 22/A 2 towards Lisbon, S. B. de Messines exit, N 124 Alte, drive left at the roundabout into the village, park at the spring park and walk up Rua dos Pisadoiros | **Tip** The parish church in the centre of Alte is a prime example of Baroque church architecture, with magnificent gilded side altars, Manueline-style elements and original *azulejo* tiles on the cross-vaulted ceiling.

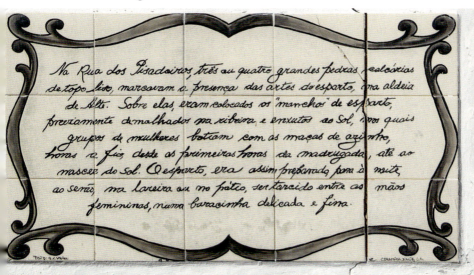

15 The Margarida Chapel
The brave peasant girl and the dragon

Once upon a time, there was a hardworking peasant girl called Margarida, who lived not far from Alte. According to local lore, one evening she was helping her mother and neighbours to gather golden esparto grass when a dragon appeared in the twilight. The girl summoned up all of her courage and looked the monster fearlessly in the eye. At this the dragon hesitated, which gave the girl time to pick up a palm frond. She approached the creature and stroked its head with the palm. The scaly intruder immediately collapsed and died, to everyone's amazement. The women were saved, the girl Margarida was sainted and the patch of land was named after her.

The Santa Margarida statue shows a barefoot young girl wrapped in a simple robe. She is holding a palm leaf in her hand, and her feet rest on the head of the dragon. However, the altar in the Margarida chapel is empty, as this figure actually stands in the right-hand altar of Alte parish church, and only visits the church on the mountain for a few days a year during the memorial service for the peasant girl. This is where the village priest used to hold the Sunday services, but the walk all the way up there was terribly hard work. And so one day the local countess called 'Enough!' She wrote a letter to the bishop in Faro complaining about the disagreeable situation; her concerns were heeded and a new parish church was built in the heart of Alte.

The little Santa Margarida church was abandoned, after falling victim first to the earthquake of 1755 and afterwards, stone by stone, to house construction in the area. Recently, locals, recalling the story of the peasant girl, have rebuilt their little church, paying for it themselves, and thus breathed new life into the Margarida cult. A winding country road connects Alte with the small settlement on the hill and leads directly to the church.

Address Largo da Igreja 1, 8100 Alte-Santa Margarida | **Getting there** Motorway junction Albufeira, A 22/A 2 towards Lisbon, S. B. de Messines exit, N 124 Alte, at the roundabout first to Alte, then turn left again straight away and follow the course of the road to Santa Margarida | **Tip** The café Água Mel on the main street in Alte awaits you, with home-made confectionery specialities and almond, fig and carob liqueurs.

ALVOR

16   The Bar at the Penina Hotel
A peace treaty that instigated a war

The Sir Henry Cotton Bar in the Penina Hotel is named after the world-class British golfer who designed the grand hotel's championship golf course. Here you can sink into worn leather armchairs and sip port from fine crystal glasses. It's a distinguished address with an appropriately stylish setting for important get-togethers. In January 1975 this was the backdrop for a meeting between the interim Portuguese government and three Angolan revolutionary leaders. The idea was to negotiate an agreement to achieve national security in Angola. For Portugal, this meeting in the Algarve should have been one of the most significant political milestones since the Carnation Revolution – the handover of the African colony, fiercely contested since 1954, was to be resolved. But that's not how things panned out.

No sooner was the provisional agreement, or *Tratado de Alvor* drawn up, than the three Angolan revolutionaries returned home. A new conflict between the Portuguese colonists, who had no intention of leaving their estates, and the indigenous people, who claimed the land as their property, began as soon as the wording of the treaty became public. The politicians protested that it was completely absurd to think that an agreement could be possible at all with such evidently contentious interests.

José de Azevedo, elected prime minister in September of the same year and an official cosignatory of the Alvor Agreement, went a step further and described the pro forma document as nothing more than a scrap of paper. As it happened, none of the partners stuck to the terms, an independence agreement never came to pass, the conflict of interests split the population into two clear camps, and the civil war that was instigated rumbled on until 2002.

Address Penina Hotel, Estrada Nacional N 125, 8501 Portimão / Alvor | **Getting there** A 22, exit 4 Alvor, N 125 towards Lagos, follow the signs for Penina Hotel | **Tip** Five minutes' drive away on the N 125 towards Lagos, a road forks off to the left to the Mexilhoeira Grande train station and leads to the end of the lagoon. Here you will find the Quinta da Rocha ornithological observation station, where you can take part in guided walks in English through the bird sanctuary, by arrangement.

17 — Lota Fish Hall
It's all about the fish

'Twenty euros – going once, going twice, going three times! The plaice go to the gentleman in the flat cap.' The hammer raps down again and again in Alvor's fishmarket hall as the day's catch is auctioned off while still on the boat. Then the rest, spread out on stone counters, is sold to housewives for pennies. At least that's how it used to be. The hall still exists, but there are no more auctions. Still, the Lota remains the symbol of the fishing community.

The fishing village of Alvor was of great importance even before the Romans arrived, thanks to the Carthaginian general Hannibal, whose campaigns took him all the way to Lusitania. Ever since, the fishing community here has shared both the catch and the risk: if there is fish, there are rewards for everyone, if not, there are none at all. The fishermen work together, repairing nets, tying thousands of hooks on long lines, skewering bait and making fish baskets. They know each other well and share each other's joy and sorrow. Most of their colourful wooden fishing boats are at least 50 years old and have belonged to the families for just as long. Late in the evening they set course for Sagres, with three or four aboard each boat, and return to Alvor in the afternoon of the following day. They unload their catch on the way to the fisheries authority in Sagres or Lagos. Back in Alvor, they go home and take a well-deserved rest, before meeting up again in the evening to watch the football in a café or to play cards and domino at the Lota.

The hall, with its wrought-iron pillars open towards the lagoon, is part of the fishermen's everyday life. At lunchtime they sup on fish soup here, in the evenings the sea dogs sit around a wobbly table, playing dominos or cards, and arguing about recent events in football. The tourists bustling every evening in the restaurants on the square out front don't bother them in the slightest.

Address Lota de Alvor, Zona da Ribeirinha, 8500 Alvor | **Getting there** A 22, exit 4, towards Alvor, then towards Zona Ribeirinha at the second roundabout in Alvor. The former fish hall is right on the shore at the end of the promenade. | **Tip** In the fishing harbour of Alvor you can watch the fishermen at work, and find out about the long-line principle or the characteristics of fish baskets.

18 The Rossio Relief
King Dom João II and Portugal's armillary sphere

In 1494, Dom João II of Portugal entered into negotiations with the Spanish king and the incumbent pope Alexander VI about where the demarcation line for the division of sovereign rights over the world's oceans should run. The Portuguese king insisted on shifting the line of longitude suggested by the Spanish a little to the west. The pope assented, Spain agreed, and the Treaty of Tordesillas was signed.

In retrospect this was a major coup for Portugal, as the realigned meridian touched the as yet undiscovered country of Brazil. The forward-looking king might have suspected that there was land on the other side of the Atlantic Ocean, but surely not how large and rich it was. And so it came to pass that in 1500 Brazil fell to Portugal, while the rest of South America came under the aegis of the Spanish conquistadors. Ever since, the meridian defined in the Treaty of Tordesillas in 1494 has encircled the middle ring of the armillary sphere on the Portuguese national flag, shiny gold and extra thick – a mystical legacy of an extraordinary episode.

On Rossio Square in Alvor there is a marble plaque carved in relief in memory of king Dom João II. He liked to visit the Algarve regularly, where he partied many nights away in Alvor with his friend, the castellan. The cunning king was in the Algarve at the end of October 1495, but unfortunately he hardly had any time for revelry, as he was overcome by a fatal fever on the very first night.

His successor Dom Manuel I ascended to the throne, assuming the freshly signed contract and with it the largest empire in history. The new king controlled maritime trade in Africa and the South Atlantic, and the sea route to India. The aforementioned meridian in the Portuguese armillary sphere is a triumphantly symbolic reminder of Dom João II and his clever tactics; the stone plaque in Alvor commemorates the date of his death.

Address Café Plaza, Largo Rossio, M 531-1, 8500 Alvor | **Getting there** A 22, exit 5 towards Alvor, turn right into the village at the roundabout and park at Rossio Square | **Tip** On the other side of the square, opposite the market hall, are the ruins of the former Moorish castle of Alvor, which was almost completely destroyed in a bloody attack by the Crusaders, known as the Massacre of 1189.

19 Ameixial Services
Doll's house atmosphere at the end of the Algarve

The Algarve comes to an end in Ameixial. The journey here from Loulé via Barranco do Velho takes you through no man's land, climbing steadily uphill in the direction of Almodôvar. Cork oak trees flank the road, their freshly husked trunks making them look as though they're wearing red socks. Here wild boar and hoopoes roam free, until the woods disperse at the pass on the edge of the village of Ameixial. The main road leads right through the middle of the spotless hamlet and is lined with beds of hydrangeas.

The village street is deserted. A solitary truck loaded with hay bales is parked on the road. The driver is having a snack in the café next to the only grocery shop in the village. The mini-supermarket is well organised and stocks all the essentials – anything else can be ordered. The standing-only café serves hearty sandwiches. The coffee machine with its six spouts, the decommissioned kitchen and unused dining hall all recall busier times in Ameixial, when the residents made a living on the back of the once bustling through traffic. Half of the villagers were employed in hospitality, and the other half in catering for the hospitality sector. Business continued to grow after the Carnation Revolution in 1974, when long-distance travellers between southern Spain and Lisbon went right through the centre of Ameixial.

The first downtime came with the construction of the IP 2 highway from Castro Marim to Beja north of the hamlet, but the definitive end of through traffic came with the completion of the A 2 Algarve–Lisbon motorway. First the petrol stations closed, then the lodgings and restaurants. The community was abandoned. Today Ameixial's main attraction is its pretty main street. The whitewashed peasant houses, with irregular natural stones left bare around the colourful windows and doors, lend the hamlet a charming doll's house atmosphere.

Address Jardim do Ameixial, state road N2 16–28, 8100 Ameixial | **Getting there** A22, exit 11, Loulé, from Loulé the N2 leads via Barranco do Velho towards Almodôvar to Ameixial | **Tip** There are many sites to discover around Ameixial, some of them accessible on hiking trails, for example the megalithic grave Anta do Beringel and the slate round house at Corte Ouro. On the way to Almodôvar you will find the Fonte da Seiceira water park as well as Moinho da Chavachã, an old watermill near Ximeno.

ARMAÇÃO DE PÊRA

20 — The Casino With No Future
Art, kitsch and curiosities

From today's perspective, the plaque commemorating the laying of the foundation stone of the old casino in Armação de Pêra reads like a cruel joke. It states that the building was specifically created for the summer visitors of the day to pass their time in what is today's beach town. And this in the era of Salazar's Second Republic, when censorship authorities completely muzzled the nation and the 'man in the street' couldn't even afford a holiday, but instead either served privileged holidaymakers from Lisbon and abroad, or worked for a pittance on *latifúndios* or in factories. Inaugurated in 1936, the casino was promoted in the propaganda of the Ministry for Art and Culture as a flagship for the nascent tourism industry on the Algarve.

The end came with the Carnation Revolution in 1974; in the course of the privatisation of formerly state-controlled businesses, the casino closed its doors. Although it is in a prime location right on the beach, the building has stood vacant ever since, and has never found a new licensee, even during the subsequent furore of chaotic urbanisation on the Algarve, in Armação de Pêra and elsewhere.

The renovation of the building was publicly advertised in 2015, but a developer has yet to be found who dares to take on the project. At least the tourist office and a hairdresser's have now moved in, and the terrace. There is an art market in the former slot-machine salon, with a hugely diverse collection of pieces begging to be browsed and rummaged. Here you will find a huge array of art and kitsch, useful and useless, classical and curious, all thrown together by an international group of artists, and more or less made in the Algarve. The first step has been taken – now brave investors for the regeneration of the remainder of the rooms must be found.

Address Casino de Armação de Pêra, Mercado Arte Artesanal, Avenida Beira-Mar, 8365 Armação de Pêra | **Getting there** A 22, exit 7, Alcantarilha, N 125 towards Albufeira, right on to N 269-1 after Alcantarilha, towards Armação de Pêra, at the first roundabout drive straight to the fishing port, park there; the casino is a five-minute walk along the beach promenade | **Hours** Daily | **Tip** Also on the beach promenade is the former defensive fort of Armação de Pêra, which has a chapel inside.

ARRIFANA

21 — The Needle Rock
A guide and protector

Arrifana is more than just an emblematic fishing port, or a picturesque village in the seclusion of the west coast. Arrifana creates a feeling of yearning. Visit once, and you'll definitely want to come back. Perhaps it's the magically sublime quality of the place, perhaps it's the people who end up here – Arrifana certainly has some kind of hypnotic attraction. The locals don't call their coast *terra santa*, 'holy land', for nothing. Here visitors can leave their daily routine far behind and find a place to relax completely. The fishing port in the Costa Vicentina nature reserve nestles in a bay in the middle of the evergreen *maquis* shrubland. Here the air always smells of juniper and the sea.

Among the surging waves at the south end of Arrifana bay, a massive rock juts out of the water. This is the fishermen's landmark, the Pedra da Agulha. When the fishermen set sail in their boats to fish, their sights are always firmly set on the needle rock – they fish using rod and line. The warriors of the sea among them leave their boats in the harbour and clamber among the rocks to collect crustaceans, or dive through waves, towering tall as houses, down into underwater grottoes in search of mussels, barnacles and slipper lobsters. Their hunting fever is like a game of roulette with the mighty ocean, with their lives as the jackpot. Like all fishermen, they also believe in protection from the heavens. For those of Arrifana, the black needle rock is the stone of Peter, on which, according to St Matthew's Gospel, Jesus built his church. That's why they revere the Pedra da Agulha as their symbol of protection.

Once a year a mass with a blessing is held for the community, from their boats at the foot of the rock. The rest of the time it serves the fishermen as a point of orientation and it is thus the key, in a figurative sense, to a safe harbour.

Address Portinho da Pesca de Arrifana, 8670 Aljezur-Arrifana | **Getting there** A 22 to Bensafrim, then towards Aljezur, turn left on to the M 1003-1 just before Aljezur towards Arrifana, park by the restaurant O Paulo on the cliffs and walk down the harbour approach | **Tip** Arrifana may make you feel you'd like to surf – if you want to try your luck, then sign up for a taster course at the surf school. At the fishing harbour you can book boat trips along the cliffs to Pedra da Agulha. Ask for Eugénio at the harbour office.

ARRIFANA

22 — Ponta da Atalaia
The chosen place of legendary Sufi knights

Ocean, sky, horizon: this is exactly what you'd imagine a chosen place to be like. In the 12th century, the legendary Sufi warriors withdrew here to the cliff promontory of Ponta da Atalaia, to pray, to found their secret society of chosen ones and to practise their initiation rites. Only 10 metres separated their mosque from the cliffs that fall away to the ocean, over 100 metres below. The altar niche of the Muslim mihrāb was oriented towards the east. When praying towards Mecca, the knights would have felt the vibrations of the breaking waves on the palms of their hands and on their foreheads.

Here they felt close to the universe, as they lit beacons and swore their unconditional allegiance to their master Ibn Qasî in the fight against invading Berber tribes. The Sufi imam, described in Arabic literature as the master in sandals, had a distinctively charismatic aura. He found it easy to win soldiers over completely, as he represented a very individual position in terms of the relationship between Muslims and Christians in Portugal at the time – he believed in peace with the Christians. That is why he sought dialogue with the first king of Portugal, invited him to the place of the chosen ones and made friends with him.

The Berbers lived in fear of Ibn Qasî and his warrior monks; it was thought that they had supernatural powers. Maybe there really was magic at play, since Sufism is after all based on the belief in spiritual energy. But perhaps the triumphant warlord was also simply a clever strategist, as he sided with the Umayyad ruler and gifted him the mosque and the chosen place for prayer on the Ponta da Atalaia. The former ribât marked the western end of the fabled Umayyad trading route that went through the Algarve towards the east, with traces from the Maghreb to Andalusia and Gibraltar, from there to North Africa and ending in Jordan.

Address Ribât de Arrifana, Ponta da Atalaia, Vale da Telha, 8670 Aljezur | **Getting there** A 22 to Bensafrim, towards Aljezur, turn left to Arrifana just before Aljezur, in Vales take a right to Vale da Telha, straight on at the next roundabout, take a left at the junction, cross two roundabouts, turn on to the sandy road and park at the end | **Tip** From the car park at Ribât, the Trilho dos Pescadores trail leads northwards along a fishermen's path and a section of the Rota Vicentina hiking route (blue/green markings) to the Monte Clérigo beach resort (4 kilometres). Cafés in Monte Clérigo serve snacks and drinks.

BARÃO DE SÃO JOÃO

23 The Cockerel Stone
Cock-a-doodle-doo from the Stone Age

In Barão São João national forest, the hustle and bustle of tourism along the coast around Lagos recedes into the far distance. Instead of the sounds of the sea and children's laughter on the beach, you will hear the wind rustling through the treetops. Birds sing. From the crest of the mountain the prospect sweeps from the Espinhaço do Cão mountain range in the west to the mountains of the Serra de Monchique to the north. On the hilltop were the remains of a citadel from over 2,000 years ago, until bulldozers came, demolished the masonry and shovelled the old stones into a pile in order to make room for half a dozen wind turbines.

Very close by you will find the trig station that marks the highest point in the Mata Nacional Barão de São João state forest. Diagonally opposite, at the crossroads, a stone with a rounded head juts out of the ground. It looks as though it was planted deep into the ground on purpose. The miniature megalith bears the evocative name Pedra do Galo, or Cockerel Stone. It dates from the Copper Age and poses quite a riddle, as it is the only one of its kind here. Standing stones usually appear in groups. According to local history, this rather squat example marks the territory of the Celtiberians, who settled in the area 3,000 years ago. The upper part is intact and did not fall victim to the Catholic Church, who set about the destruction of all heathen effigies during the *Reconquista*.

This may be due to the superstition that surrounds the stone. An old story says that anyone who hears the sound of a cockerel crowing there – a cock-a-doodle-doo from the Stone Age – isn't long for this world. Or it may simply be because the megalith was never discovered, here in the middle of the woods. What is quite sure, however, is that a cockerel has never been seen near the megalith, never mind heard – though who would live to confirm this?

Address Perímetro Florestal Mata Nacional de Barão de São João, 8600 Lagos | **Getting there** A22 to Bensafrim, N120 towards Lagos, on exiting Bensafrim turn right towards Barão de São João on the N535, then follow the signs to Mata Nacional de Barão de São João | **Tip** If you follow Estrada Barão São João you will get to Espiche, and then via the N125 to Praia da Luz on the coast. From there the M537 will take you to Burgau, and further on an unnamed clifftop road to the ruins of Forte de Almadena, the beach at Boca do Rio and then Salema.

BENAFIM

24 The Ara Vitae Sculpture
Borges' search for the cradle of humanity

The last thing a visitor to the isolated hamlet of Benafim would expect to see is a bronze sculpture depicting a bare-breasted naked woman emerging from the centre of a globe, cracked open in two like an egg. *Ara Vitae* (Latin for 'altar of life') is the legacy of a unique character from Benafim who went out into the world to search for the location of the cradle of humanity. Before he could finish presenting his extensive theories about this in written form, he was torn from life by illness. The creator of the sculpture, Victor Borges, was born in Benafim. He studied in France, and worked in the USA before returning home to Barrocal to work as an architect. But Borges wasn't only an architect: he was a man of letters, and a sculptor with a penchant for the experimental, but above all he was a scrutiniser.

He never took historical facts as given, but always dug deeper and through this persistence he continually arrived at new theories, which he expressed through his work. After his death in 2012, he left extensive notes on the Bible and its encrypted messages, as well as an unfinished manuscript on the subject. The piece was finished by friends and colleagues, and published posthumously by Arandis Editora under the title *Apokalypsis*. In this work, Borges scrutinises events and episodes from the Bible and provides his own answers to the question of the origin of Christianity.

After Borges' death, the *Ara Vitae* statue, which had stood since 1995 in the city of Loulé, was moved back home to Benafim. It was erected on the village square, in a formal ceremony with prayers for its creator. With its message of love and feminine omnipresence, the naked woman and her resurrection from the middle of the earth can be understood as a comment on the conventional patriarchy, and at the same time as an illustration of Borges' theory on the cradle of humanity.

Address Rua das Bicas Velhas 70–72, 8100 Benafim | **Getting there** A2 towards Lisbon, exit S. B. de Messines, N 124 Alte towards Salir, turn left in Benafim on to Rua Sá Carneiro, follow Rua das Bicas Velha to the end | **Tip** An exploratory tour through Benafim leads past the old public washhouse to the parish church of St Mary Glória and the chapel in honour of Our Lady of Fátima. Four kilometres' drive away is the resort of Quinta de Freixo (birthplace of Victor Borges) which has a wildlife park.

BENSAFRIM

25_ The Bensafrim Stone
An upside-down message

Though Bensafrim certainly has the nostalgic patina of a little Algarve village, there are no 'major' attractions waiting to be discovered here. The heart of the hamlet is to be found in the twisting alleyways beyond the main street, and their charm is quite seductive. Some of the façades are built so close together that you can only get through the narrow passages on foot. A row of peasant houses, some of them over 200 years old, are clustered together between the parish church and the old village threshing floor. The outer walls have been painted over so many times that you can actually count the layers of whitewash. If you follow the street uphill, you reach Bensafrim's market place with its local council office, market hall and pharmacy.

Next to the pharmacy is a park planted with a ring of deodar cedars, an evergreen tree whose cones smell of pepper. In the centre stands a glass vitrine containing a slab of red sandstone. The stone panel measures around one metre tall, 60 centimetres wide and two hands thick. Characters that resemble letters are engraved on the stone. These words from remote antiquity and their message are more than 2,000 years old; they are evidence that the advanced Celtiberian culture that was present in the region at that time was already using its own written language.

However, the panel here in the park is in fact a replica. After vandals covered the original with obscene drawings, the real Bensafrim stone was replaced by this one. The original is now in northern Portugal, housed in the Santos Rocha Municipal Museum in Figueira da Foz. Experts in ancient scripts will be able to decipher the message straight away, as an inscription for the grave of a prominent figure from the area. They will also immediately realise, from the order of the characters, that the replica stone was actually installed upside down.

Address Rua de João de Deus 19, 8600 Bensafrim | **Getting there** A 22 to Bensafrim, take the first exit to the right on the motorway roundabout, turn left before the lights and park; the park is next to the pharmacy | **Tip** Five minutes' walk away, at the other end of the village, the Campinhos pub welcomes you in for a rest and a snack. Beneath the mousetraps, bottle gourds and antique instruments that decorate the place, the Bifana schnitzel sandwich tastes particularly good. A 10-minute drive in the direction of Lagos/Sargoçal on the M-535-1 will take you to the organic vineyard of Monte da Casteleja.

BOLIQUEIME

26 The New Village School
Petrol station owner's son becomes president

The primary school in Boliqueime is named Escola Básica Integrada Professor Doutor Aníbal Cavaco Silva, in honour of the former president of Portugal. Cavaco Silva grew up in Boliqueime as the son of the owner of a petrol station. He was a pupil here in the former village school, then studied economics at university. From initially working simply as a regular member of the Social Democratic Party of Portugal (PSD), Cavaco Silva ended up having quite a stellar political career. He directed Portugal's political interests for a total of 20 years – 10 years as prime minister followed by a further 10 as president.

In 1985, Cavaco Silva entered parliament as the election winner for the first time, replacing Mário Soares' cabinet and guiding Portugal into the European Union. With its entry into the EU, the country enjoyed an enormous economic upturn and was soon bedded into the European market structure. Cavaco Silva seized the post of head of state in 2006, and was in office until 2016, when he was replaced by the current incumbent, Marcelo Rebelo de Sousa. Former president Cavaco Silva was considered a dyed-in-the-wool conservative, his public demeanour of always remaining aloof ran strictly according to protocol, and he came across as stiff and old-fashioned rather than urbane, especially at state receptions.

During the brutal austerity that the Passos–Coelho government oversaw from 2011 to 2015, Cavaco Silva once declared that he couldn't cover his monthly personal expenses on his salary as president, and that he was very glad he also received a professor's pension. To the Portuguese people this remark was like a slap in the face, as the average monthly salary for the working class in Portugal is still well below €1,000 before tax. His political legacy, partly positive, partly negative, has continued to reverberate since his replacement.

Address Escola Básica Integrada, Rua da Escola, 8700 Boliqueime | **Getting there** A 22, exit 10, N 270 Boliqueime, turn right on to Rua da Escola before the roundabout. The petrol station that belonged to Cavaco Silva's father (long since under new management) is west of Boliqueime on the N 125 | **Tip** In the hinterland of Boliqueime is the farming village of Tôr with its Roman bridge, the Santa Rita hermitage and the Quinta da Tôr vineyard. Not far from Tôr is the hamlet of Querença, which has a Baroque church and a Museum of Water.

BORDEIRA

27 — The Accordion Capital
The soul of folk music is in Bordeira

In the Algarve folk scene Bordeira is considered the cradle and capital of accordion music. 'Keep twirling – don't stop!' Faster and faster, the dancing couples spin each other around, leaping across the dance floor and at the same time stamping feet in three-four time. The accordion drives the dancing on, the dancers spur on the musicians, the tempo accelerates to a brilliantly merry finale. The best-known Algarve folk dance is called the *corridinho*. It originated in Bordeira, it's fun and easy to learn – and it isn't even 100 years old. The accordion has only played a part in local folk music since the 1920s, and probably first made its way to the Algarve with soldiers returning from World War I. Sustained by the constant readiness of the people to socialise, the instrument is a particularly good fit here, where it is seen as *alma algarvia*, the soul of Algarve folk music.

The first two nationally recognised Portuguese accordionists, José Ferreiro and João Bexiga, both came from Bordeira. The two thoroughbred musicians were virtuosos of their instrument, who left the folk music scene with more than 200 pieces of music for accordion. Several musicians have emerged from their tradition and made the folk music of the Algarve famous throughout the country, with the instrument that can laugh and cry at the same time.

Another musical tradition to be found in Bordeira is that of the *charolas*. In an act of solidarity with those in need, musicians go from door to door on New Year's Eve and Epiphany (6 January), playing instruments and singing, and are rewarded with food and money. At the end of the tour the musicians split the money they've collected and give it away. The veneration of the village community for their two exponents of the accordion is reflected in two streets that run right through the hamlet, which bear the names of the musicians.

Address Caminho João Barra Bexiga / Rua José Ferreiro Pai, 8005 Bordeira | **Getting there** A 22, exit 14, N 2 towards São Bras de Alportel, after the motorway turn left on to the EM 523 and follow it to Bordeira | **Tip** The accordion and its music feature regularly at Bordeira's cultural centre. For more information check the Faro city portal online. Ten minutes' drive from Bordeira is Santa Bárbara de Nexe, a 14th-century church with an amazingly elaborate ribbed vault above the main altar.

BORDEIRA

28 The Os Agostos Estate
Chamber music with nibbles in the barn

Shortly after the Carnation Revolution, the Algarve was in economic slumber and a cultural deep sleep. The beauty of this south-west corner of Europe had not yet been 'discovered'; the coastal area dozed in its nostalgic cocoon of decaying glory and had only experienced a new economic stimulus in the holiday destinations of Albufeira, Quarteira, Vilamoura and Praia da Rocha. There were no cultural activities, save religious processions and village fêtes. Prompted by the idea of creating a place for culture and interaction for the foreign diaspora already resident here, a handful of English and German residents founded the São Lourenço cultural centre in Almancil as a point of contact for artists and art lovers.

Just a short while later, the idea inspired a second group of culturally engaged, like-minded lovers of classical music, to establish their own association, the Assoçiação dos Amigos da Música de São Lourenço. Their ambitious aim was and still is to invite world-class musicians from all over the globe to give chamber concerts in intimate surroundings on the Algarve. Piers Lane from Australia, Katya Apekisheva from Russia, Sa Chen from China and Alexander Schimpf from Germany are some of the outstanding names from the long list of top-class chamber musicians whom the expat Algarve audience have had the honour to hear in concert over more than 25 years.

Helga Hampton, the chair, is by all accounts picky in her selection of musicians, but its success should give her every right to remain so. The 16 concerts organised every year in the former barn on the Os Agostos estate near Santa Bárbara de Nexe are always completely sold out to the very last seat. Delicious finger food is served before the concert and in the interval. The estate has a stylish 18th-century farmstead which you can visit or rent for family parties, big or small.

Address Quinta Os Agostos, Sítio dos Agostos, 8005 Santa Bárbara de Nexe, www.amigos-de-musica.org | **Getting there** A 22, exit 13, Faro, exit Estadio do Algarve, left at first roundabout, straight on at second roundabout to Santa Bárbara de Nexe, follow signs in the village to Bordeira, turn right to Agostos, and after 100 metres left to the estate | **Tip** Ten minutes' drive away from Os Agostos is Estoi, with its Rococo Palácio de Estoi, the Roman ruins at Milreu and the hill of Cerro do Guilhim, which has an outlook area on the summit.

CACELA VELHA

29 The Factory Beach
A touch of the South Seas on the Algarve

The Algarve coastal village of Cacela Velha, at the eastern end of the Ria Formosa nature reserve, is still an insider tip for its almost deserted beaches, even at the height of summer. This is partly to do with the fact that there are no island-hopping ferry services here, nor anyone renting out beach loungers, and the sandbanks can only be reached by rowing boat, water taxi or a long walk. A paradise within reach, but only after a bit of effort is expended. Among the locals, the beach is known by the highly unromantic name of 'the factory beach'. The image that calls to mind is of smoking chimneys, clattering machines and trucks driving back and forth. But there is none of that – the factory has closed, and instead an opulent villa looks down from the dunes.

The Praia da Fábrica is a real-life dream beach – you might even imagine yourself far from the Algarve coast, far from Portugal, far from Europe, somewhere on an atoll in the middle of the South Seas. As fine as icing sugar, the sandbank islands glow, their shapes changing with the tide, opal green shimmering seawater lapping on their shores. On the seabed octopuses stalk around, crabs dart to and fro. There are no jet skis growling, and not even a vendor of *bolas de Berlim* to disturb the tranquility or the views of the former fortress and the church of Cacela Velha.

Wooden boats bob up and down between island, beach and village, with mussel farmers rowing to their harvesting sites in the lagoon or taking sun worshippers to the islands. If you walk along the coast a little, you'll be able to enjoy a view of one of the 15 most beautiful beaches in the world, as selected by *Condé Nast Traveller* magazine. The route there leads you on foot through the picturesque but sleepy village of Cacela Velha and past the ruins of a former pottery factory, after which this beach paradise is named.

Address Rua de Fábrica, Cacela Velha, 8900 Vila Nova de Cacela | **Getting there** A 22, exit 16, N 270 Tavira, N 125 Vila Real de Santo António, in Nora turn right on to the M 1242, then right on to Rua de Fábrica just before Cacela Velha; car park by the beach | **Tip** To the north of the N 125 is the forested region of Conceição da Tavira, with an extensive network of walking routes and a bathing lake. Within walking distance, or a short car journey towards the west is the citadel of São João da Barra.

CARRAPATEIRA

30 The Land and Sea Museum
Where the farmers are fishermen too

The N 268 stretches for 14 kilometres parallel to the west coast, from Vila do Bispo to Carrapateira in the north. Just before Carrapateira, the access road to the legendary surf beach of Praia do Amado forks off to the left. In town and to the right is the market square with shops, post office, cafés and surfing businesses. Sand dunes and hills dotted with bungalows and gardens loom up to the left, towards the sea. The phenomenally large Carrapateira bay begins behind the dunes. Endless spume-capped waves wash in, sunlight dances in the haze of sea water. As far as the eye can see is sand, sand and more sand.

It seems like a desert on the Atlantic, but this impression is deceptive. The people who live in and around Carrapateira are busy farmers. They cultivate fields in the floodplain behind their village on the other side of the main road and in the dunes. And they know what they're doing. Peanuts, sweet potatoes, broad beans, pumpkins and cabbage are among the crops that thrive here in the sand. In fact, there are more farmers than fishermen in Carrapateira. Fishing, which is generally the main source of income elsewhere in the Algarve, was only done for subsistence here until about 20 years ago. It was only when surfers and backpackers began to discover south-west Portugal that fishing and harvesting seafood became profitable enterprises here.

Since then most farmers have worked as fishermen in the morning and in agriculture in the afternoon, which has earned them the nickname of 'amphibians' among their countrymen. The community museum, Museu do Mar e da Terra, sits atop the hill at the end of the road beyond the church. Here you can gain a detailed insight into the work of the farmer-fishermen, and wander through an impressive photographic display on the coast's underwater world. The best view over Carrapateira and the beach is included in the price.

Address Museu do Mar e da Terra, Rua do Estado 1, 8670 Bordeira, Carrapateira | **Getting there** A 22, exit 1, N 125 towards Sagres, in Vila do Bispo take the N 268 towards Aljezur, park in Carrapateira and walk to the museum | **Hours** Tue – Sat 10am – 1pm & 1.30 – 5pm | **Tip** Carrapateira's two main beaches, Praia do Amado and Praia de Carrapateira / Bordeira are stunners. The sand track that runs between them takes you very close to the cliffs, past the fishing port of Portinho do Forno and the archaeological excavation site of an ancient fishing village.

CARVOEIRO

31 The DEKA Community Centre
Ecumenical services with the sound of the sea

The double doors of the chapel on the cliffs are always wide open on Sundays. Sunlight streams through the portal in the snug nave of the church, dancing between the wooden pews, over the worn stone tiles, and brushing the plain marble altar. The priest reads from his sermon and the congregation sings the appropriate hymn. A church service celebrated like anywhere else in the Western Christian world, you might think, and yet this service is different. The congregation in the parish church of Our Lady of the Incarnation in Carvoeiro isn't that of a normal Catholic parish. The church is also home to the German-speaking Evangelical Lutheran Congregation of the Algarve, known as DEKA for short.

As an offshoot from Lisbon, this branch on the Algarve was created over 25 years ago on the initiative of the German honorary consul at that time, Enzo von Baselli, along with his wife Catarina and a handful of their fellow German-speaking Protestant residents. Together they wanted to offer a meeting place for believers of various denominations and different countries of origin, as well as a place of spiritual support. The bishop of Faro enthusiastically agreed to the innovative request for the parallel use of a church building by Catholics and Protestants, and granted DEKA unlimited permission to use the Catholic-dedicated church of Ermida Nossa Senhora da Encarnação alongside Carvoeiro's Catholic congregation.

The ecumenical project on the Algarve rapidly took shape and it has now established itself as an institution with an open door for locals, residents and tourists of various denominations. The parish priest takes care of Sunday services, Holy Communion and discussion groups, and organises baptisms and weddings by arrangement.

Address Ermida Nossa Senhora da Encarnação, Rampa Senhora Encarnação 29, 8400 Carvoeiro, www.deka.com | **Getting there** A 22, exit 6, exit Lagoa south, go towards Carvoeiro, follow the signs for Algar Seco; the church is on the right at the end of the street | **Hours** Open for visits Sept–June, Tue 3.30–5pm | **Tip** Park at the Algar Seco cave complex and visit the sea caves in the cliffs on a boat trip with the tour organiser Carvoeiro Caves.

CASTRO MARIM

32_ The Salt Spa
Bathing in sea salt for well-being

From its source at the Ojos del Guadiana in Castile-La Mancha, the Guadiana river crosses the Spanish Extremadura, separating the two Iberian countries before emptying into the Atlantic Ocean at Vila Real de Santo António. Here, fresh water and salt water flow into each other with the action of the tide. Twice a day the seawater pushes up the Guadiana into the tributaries that branch out like fine capillaries all around the medieval stronghold of Castro Marim. Between these channels fields stretch out, some large and many small, laid out in regular rectangles – these are salt basins that are naturally filled with seawater by the force of gravity. During the hot summer months, the water in these basins, or salt pans, slowly concentrates through evaporation.

In the district of Castro Marim, the white gold of antiquity has been a pillar of the indigenous economy for over 2,500 years, and it has guaranteed work and a salary for the local population continuously ever since. The coveted sea salt continues to be produced naturally and sustainably here. A daily portion of salt is essential for the survival of the human organism, and there should be a place for natural sea salt in every kitchen, as an extra pinch of something different. But sea salt from the Algarve has more to offer than simply acting as an exquisite seasoning – as you will be sure to find out at the Agua Mãe salt pans.

Here you can paddle in natural salt basins as the fancy takes you, through saltwater and mud, or have a leisurely float in brine. The Agua Mãe sea salt spa uses this natural phenomenon to offer its customers salt baths during the summer months, alongside exfoliating scrubs with *flor de sal*, massage and yoga. You can also enjoy organic snacks, smoothies and herbal teas, while salt workers harvest sea salt close by. It's a unique place to turn off and enjoy being pampered.

Address Agua Mãe Spa Salina Barquinha, Estrada Nacional N 122, 8950 Castro Marim, www.facebook.com/aguamae.cm | **Getting there** A 22, exit 18, N 122 Castro Marim, turn left at the second roundabout on to the gravel road and follow the signs for Agua Mãe | **Hours** May–Sept; check Facebook page for times | **Tip** A circular hiking trail leads through the middle of the Sapal de Castro Marim nature reserve to the saltworks around Castro Marim, and further on to the Centro de Interpretação Sapal nature centre. By car, the nature reserve is reached from a turn-off on the N 122 / IC 27 that forks to the right into marshland just after the motorway approach road.

CASTRO MARIM

33_ The Symbol of the Castle
A medieval knight welcomes you

A knight in armour with lance, shield and the cross of the Order of Christ on his chain mail welcomes drivers to Castro Marim. He's not a real knight of course, but rather a life-size impression of one, a figure created in openwork steel mounted on a horse crafted from steel loops. The four-metre-tall sculpture, which stands in the middle of a roundabout, is from hoof to lance-tip made out of scrap metal. The artist Carlos Correia first discovered his affinity with creative metallurgy when he was wondering what to do with the metal waste that was left over from his work as a landscape gardener.

Fascinated by working with fire and anvil, he now creates monumental sculptures, each bigger than the last. Correia never wanted to make abstract art, and he specialised in representational work from the very beginning, with pieces interpreting the traditions and crafts of his Algarve homeland. But soon the static format that he'd begun with was no longer enough for him – he felt that his creations were empty. After several attempts to lend his figures more dynamism, Correia began to add relevant attributes to his sculptures. So the knight of Castro Marim is complete with horse, shield and lance, just as the cork stripper from Silves has a donkey in tow. You will now find Correia's work in several towns, and each piece stands out in its own way through its individual character. Decoration alone is not enough for this artist – for each location he selects a protagonist appropriate to the history of the place. So the knight of the Order of Christ can immediately be seen to represent the former importance of Castro Marim's medieval castle, as a defensive post on the fluid border with Spain – he is in just the right place here. The castle has been disused since the time of the Napoleonic invasion, and is now resurrected only for the annual medieval festival and pageant.

Address Estatua do Cavaleiro Medieval, Rua 25 de Abril 121, 8950 Castro Marim | **Getting there** A 22, exit 18, the N 122 leads directly to the roundabout with the knight | **Tip** Castro Marim is a medieval fortified city with two castles, and the Knights Templars' castle of Santiago is open to visitors. The church of Our Lady of Martyrs is also worth a visit. A Casa do Sal is a museum where you can find out all there is to know about the production of sea salt, and in Revelim do Santo António you can learn more about the ecology of the Guadiana riverbanks.

CONCEIÇÃO DE TAVIRA

34_ The Beach Fortress
An extra guard for the tuna

The only citadel on the Algarve coast built in the style of the French military architect Vauban that is still standing can be found on the beach of Cabanas de Tavira. Like all Vauban's strongholds, this one was considered impregnable, and its quadratic ground plan, like those at Lille in France or Elvas in Portugal, is impressive. Here too a tower at each corner of the fortress protrudes sharply to form a star shape if viewed from above. Hidden behind the imposing external wall is a corridor and a second, lower barricade, which is now filled with earth and serves as a walkway. Inside the fortress is the former drill ground, now a neatly mown lawn; in its centre is the former governor's palace. This perfectly constructed stronghold in the midst of the sand dunes near Cabanas de Tavira was built around 1640, during the war that the Portuguese fought against Spain to regain national sovereignty, which rumbled on for almost 30 years. The citadel was actually involved in three military conflicts: against the Spanish on the road to the Iberian Union, then against Napoleon's maritime invasion, and finally during the Civil War. Also known as the War of the Two Brothers, this was between the royal siblings Dom Miguel, who wanted to reintroduce autocratic monarchy, and Dom Pedro IV, who was in favour of continuing the constitutional form of government.

Later, the fort fulfilled a completely different purpose. The soldiers were charged with guarding the *armação de atum*, tuna fish traps set up off the coast. These were regularly raided and plundered by fishing fleets from Spain, Scandinavia and Morocco, and the valuable tuna fish stolen. Now there are no more traps in Tavira, and the stronghold is in private hands. The lovingly renovated former governor's palace is today home to a country hotel. On the battlements, deckchairs recline in the shade of palm trees.

Address Forte de São João da Barra, Sitio da Fortaleza, 8800 Cabanas de Tavira, www.fortesaojoaodabarra.com | **Getting there** A 22, exit 16, N 270 Tavira, N 125 towards Vila Real de Santo António, in Conceição de Tavira turn right to Cabanas and follow the signs to Forte da Barra | **Tip** The Passadiço de Cabanas promenade begins and ends at the harbour at the other end of Cabanas de Tavira. The boardwalk offers a wide selection of fish restaurants and cafés with a laid-back maritime flair, and views of the lagoon.

35 — The Grotto of Venus
Three delightful nymphs and their Zeus

The pink Belle Époque castle in Estoi looks uncannily similar to the royal palace of Queluz in the eponymous upper-class suburb of Lisbon. This should come as no surprise, as it was none other than the royal court architect Mateus de Oliveira, designer of the original in Lisbon, who also built this smaller version in Estoi, following his own template. The manor is *the* Rococo pearl in the Algarve, and in its time it was a prestigious locale for the chief commander in the Algarve. Today the noble country estate houses a hotel.

As you wander through the rooms, it is quite easy to imagine how the emissaries of Napoleon Bonaparte dined here. Furnished with a variety of works of art and furniture from the period of Louis XIV, the Palácio de Estoi clearly reflects the era of opulence among the Portuguese aristocracy of the 19th century. For the local population, the palace offered a multitude of secure jobs, and the park next to it was a place of refined recreation. Among its most impressive features are the gallery of marble busts, in the only Versailles-style box hedge garden in the Algarve, the Roman portico and the sensual, erotic mural in the west pavilion. An imposing flight of stairs, decorated with fountains, marble sculptures and tiled panels, leads from the box hedge garden into the large park, via an archway and a private road.

A fanciful fountain grotto is hidden under the steps. Seen as a place of leisure from the beginning, the grotto is richly decorated with mosaic art and faience. The fountain, with its three goddesses of love, perfectly modelled and with delightful smiles, creates a space with a decidedly lascivious mood. This is where the ladies of the court once met to chat, compose love letters and exchange secrets; now it is a place for lovers. The palace and the park are accessible even if you're not a guest of the hotel.

Address Pousada Palácio de Estoi, Rua de São José 13, 8005 Estoi-Faro | **Getting there** A 22, exit 14, towards Estoi, follow signs to Pousada Palácio de Estoi | **Tip** Walk through Pé da Cruz, the mule-coach quarter of Estoi, and you'll go through two centuries of architectural history. On the bridge before the Estoi motorway junction is a café with a rooftop terrace and a fantastic view of the palace. Just past the bridge on the left are the excavations of the Roman villa of Milreu.

ESTÔMBAR

36 — The Escape Route
Race for justice on a three-wheeler

The British comedy-drama *The Right Juice* premiered in 2013, and won an award at the 2014 International Edmonton Film Festival. The film begins with a failed city banker called Oliver who leaves everything in London behind, moves to the Algarve and invests his entire savings in a remote farm in the hills of Silves. Here he dreams of a life in charge of an orange plantation, with his wife Sally as the orange princess. However, she is far from impressed by the derelict farm cottage and the rural lifestyle, and soon returns to London. Oliver stays, rolls up his sleeves, and plants every orange tree seedling himself.

His nearest neighbour knows from the start that Oliver will fail, as his land has no water supply. Their mutual third neighbour, Andreus, has literally turned off the tap by creating a private reservoir. He is hoping that Oliver will give up and sell the land to him at a knock-down price, so that he can then sell it on at a huge profit to a hotel consortium. But things don't get that far. Oliver enrols the help of car mechanic Manel and his neighbour Nesta, who is also being put under pressure to sell her mother's house.

This feel-good comedy was the first English-language feature film entirely shot in the Algarve. Its British and Portuguese cast bring together all of the clichés about life as a foreigner in the Algarve, and it is precisely this that makes it laugh-out-loud funny. Just as in real life, the protagonists are saved by a clause in the country's legislation about public rights to water. Of course, they still have to fight for it. Oliver's race for his rights begins with a frantic chase, with the three friends in a motorised three-wheeler, through the backstreets of Estômbar, past the church and Largo do Castelo square, zigzagging through narrow passageways and down Rua de Ibn'Ammar at high speed towards the high street.

Address Largo do Castelo/Rua de Ibn'Ammar, 8400 Estômbar | Getting there A 22, exit 6, towards Lagoa south, right at the first roundabout, turn right after the level crossing to Estombâr and follow the signs to Igréja | Tip Estômbar's cemetery and the open staircase in front of the church offer the best view of the steel-cable bridge over the Arade river.

ESTÔMBAR

37 — The Grotto of the Vizier
Secret tunnel of caliphs and kings

The entrance to the Gruta de Ibn'Ammar is closed off by an iron grille. For good reason – you certainly shouldn't explore these caves without the right equipment, including a helmet, and are best off booking a guided tour. You enter through the confined space of a tunnel, which slowly grows in size until the grotto opens up and discloses its treasures of stony stalactites and stalagmites. Underground lakes capture the echo of whispered words. According to an oft-told legend, the cave passages lead from here all the way to Silves, and once helped a Moorish caliph to escape from the castle or, alternatively, to enter it unnoticed. Ibn'Ammar, the son of a shepherd from Estômbar, knew the caves like the back of his hand. He would often escape here in order to write – he wanted to be a poet, not a goatherd.

His extraordinary poetic talent led Ibn'Ammar to Seville and the caliph's palace, where he won the trust of Prince Al-Mu'tamid. During their assault on Silves, Ibn'Ammar led the prince and his soldiers through the caves of Estômbar into the heart of the old royal city, and Al-Mu'tamid conquered the castle in an instant. The new king of Silves appointed his friend grand vizier, and christened the magical cave Gruta de Ibn'Ammar in his honour.

One hundred years later, during the invasion of the Portuguese Crusaders under King Sanchez II, the very same secret passage helped the feared King Almansor of Morocco and his soldiers to flee the besieged castle unnoticed, in a battle known as the Massacre of 1189. Almansor and his men escaped to Estômbar, and from there stalked back to Silves, taking the Crusaders completely by surprise. As the new caliph of Silves, Seville and Cordoba, Almansor forced the Catholic conquerors out of the Algarve to the north, and only ended his campaign of revenge with the capture of the Templar castle of Tomar.

Address Gruta de Ibn'Ammar, Rua dos Arrais, 8400 Estômbar, Lagoa | **Getting there** A 22, exit 6, towards Lagoa south, then towards Estômbar, turn right on to the second road after the level crossing and follow the signs to Gruta de Ibn'Ammar; park by the bridge | **Hours** A private guided tour of the caves, in English and including equipment, can be booked with Carlos Filipe at Centro Estudos Subterrâneos in Lagos; lagos.ces@gmail.com | **Tip** Between Lagoa and Estômbar is the Slide and Splash water park, with fun slides down from scary heights.

ESTÔMBAR

38_ The Spring-water Park
Splashy fun in summer or winter

Hidden in a broad overflowing tributary of the Arade river, the Sítio das Fontes park is an idyllic oasis with a forest and a natural open-air swimming pond, not far from the coast. Reeds and sea grass grow on the banks of the pool. Water plants and lilies give the lagoon a tropical atmosphere. The natural springs are set up as an ecological leisure park, with a picnic area and amphitheatre for concerts and other events, all around the former tidal mill on the banks of the lagoon. You can swim in the pond, and watch the frogs, with a view of the secluded floodplain.

The water in the pond is fresh and its temperature stays constant, whether it's summer or winter. It comes from the Algarve's largest aquifer, via underground springs that ceaselessly squeeze groundwater to the surface, bubbling up through the porous rock – a natural phenomenon that occurs in areas extremely rich in limestone, in terrain known as karst. The watermill in the former miller's house has been restored. It houses an ethnographic exhibition with antique agricultural tools, and is usually open for a few hours on Sundays. Beneath the miller's house, the incoming tide once powered a bucket wheel, which in its turn, by way of cogwheels, rotated the two impressive millstones in the mill. The implements exhibited show how farmers in the Algarve cultivated their fields and harvested cereals in previous centuries.

Next to the mill, an arched bridge spanning the bathing pond leads the way to the children's playground. The main Arade river can be reached by a shady walk through a nearby forest, with a nature trail and various keep-fit areas along the way. Locals as well as foreign residents meet here at Sítio das Fontes for picnics and barbecues. If you'd rather be undisturbed on your visit to the park, come during the week and get here nice and early – you'll have the oasis all to yourself.

Address Parque Municipal do Sítio das Fontes, Estrada Intermunicipal, 8400 Lagoa/Estômbar | **Getting there** A 22, exit 6, N 124 Lagoa-south towards Estômbar; in Estômbar follow the main road towards Silves for about 2.5 kilometres, then left to Sítio das Fontes | **Tip** A boat trip from Portimão to Silves takes almost four hours, with a break in Silves. With the solar-powered pleasure boat Alvor Flor de Sol, you float through the fascinating river landscape to the Moorish royal city without the constant noise of a petrol-driven motor (alvorboattrips.com).

39 — The Grain Barn
The Greek riddle of Faro

After travelling on stormy seas for months on end, the Greek adventurer Ulysses arrived one day in the calm waters of a river estuary, and christened the settlement on its banks Olissippo. The safe harbour at the end of his odyssey was what today is Lisbon. Whether the legendary protagonist of Homer's epic poem (and inspiration for James Joyce's novel) was ever in Faro in the Algarve remains unclear. Nevertheless, the fabled seafarer is clearly recognisable on the front of a former watchtower, an octagonal building in a residential area in the city centre. Ulysses stands resplendent on a five-metre-high stone relief, sculpted on the wall of a half-collapsed tower that doesn't attract much attention, either from its neighbours or from passing tourists.

This was the largest of a total of six bastions on the Cerca Seiscentista, the 17th-century city wall. It served as a defence against advancing Spanish invaders, and protected the citizens of Faro from Napoleon's infantry. There is no door in the tower; a staircase that climbs the façade leads up into it. The watchtower in Faro was inspired by the Tower of the Winds in Athens, and it is unique in Portugal in its octagonal form. In the 19th century it became obsolete as a military post. A tiled roof was affixed to its crenellations, and thenceforth it served as a barn for the Franciscan monks in the Convento de São Francisco.

The tower is currently walled in on a private piece of land, but you can see Ulysses from the side street of Rua Sport Faro Benfica, or from the cul-de-sac behind the tower. He is holding a trident in his left hand and a defeated reptile in his right. Other figures from Greek mythology, Neptune for example, can be made out on the tower's other faces. Unfortunately these other reliefs are crumbling away on the dilapidated building, and might well soon disappear without trace.

Address Torre Seiscentista, Rua Sport Faro Benfica/Rua Manuel Panteado 24, 8000 Faro | **Getting there** A 22, exit 13, Faro Centro, follow the signs for the Vila-a-Dentro to the São Francisco car park; on foot from Rua Caçadores Quatro, turn right into Rua Sport Faro Benfica | **Tip** The São Francisco church is impressive, with its frescoes and painted tile panels, most notably one showing a rare motif of Francis of Assisi, who symbolically props up the tilting Catholic Church with his shoulder.

40_ The Jewish Cemetery
Portugal's first printed book

Faro's Jewish cemetery is located near both the football stadium and the hospital. Eighteen cypress trees – planted as a symbolic number for eternal life – grow here around the graves. The wrought-iron gate is open to anyone who wishes to enter with peaceful intent. The plain graves in the cemetery are covered with stone slabs, on which the names of the dead and the dates of their deaths are engraved in Hebraic script. Pebbles line the borders of the gravestones. Each pebble symbolises a very personal greeting to the deceased from individual surviving relatives.

The history of the city of Faro is closely connected with the history of the Sephardic Jews on the Algarve. The former Jewish quarter with its shops and workshops spread out around the Lethes Theatre in what is today the Alagoa quarter. The Jewish publisher Samuel Gacon had his office here, with a workshop next door. Gacon earned a place in both local and national history when in 1487 he created the first-ever printed book in Portugal, an *incunabulum* of the first five books of the Old Testament. The original copy of what is now known as the Faro Pentateuch, made up of 110 pages in Hebraic script, is a rarity whose value is beyond price. With the printing of the Pentateuch, the Jewish publisher and master printer Gacon laid the foundations of book printing, and for a completely new era of reproduction and dissemination of literature and printed matter in Portugal.

In 1596, the English general Robert Devereux, Earl of Essex, led a raid on Faro during the struggles that led up to the Iberian Union. Part of the booty he stole, to present to his beloved Queen Elizabeth I, was Gacon's *incunabulum*. Today, the first book ever printed in Portugal is kept in the British Library in London. A privately curated exhibition at the cemetery gives more information about the history of the Jews in Faro.

Address Cemitério Judaico de Faro, Estrada da Penha 38, 8000 Faro | **Getting there** A 22, exit 13, Faro Centro, in Faro towards Olhão and stadium, park in front of the cemetery | **Hours** Mon–Fri 9.30am–12.30pm & 2–5pm | **Tip** A few minutes' walk away is the Baroque church Igréja do Carmo, which has the second-biggest chapel of bones in Portugal. The Mercado Municipal market hall and Faro's high street, with its chic pedestrianised zone, are also nearby.

41 The Obelisk of Faro
Portugal's most famous slap in the face

They say that when an Italian gets stuck in Portugal, it's probably because of love. But in the late 19th century it was the political freedom of Faro that lured the Italian Nicolau Canivari here. The mild climate was also good for him, he liked the cheery mood of the people and the cuisine was good. There was only one thing he missed from his homeland: a decent café, where you could read the paper, smoke a cigar and sip at your coffee. Driven by his own nostalgia, Canivari opened the first coffee house in Faro, which quickly developed into an intercultural meeting place, a centre both for intellectual exchange and the deepening of business and political ties. It was here that a minister of the royal upper chamber, José Bento Ferreira de Almeida, and the Italian coffee house owner met for the first time. They soon became rapt in conversation about art and politics.

Canivari admired the highly decorated naval commander and founder of the naval college in Faro for his political straightforwardness. This had once almost cost Almeida his honour. He wanted the practice of corporal punishment in the navy to be abolished, as he found it deeply humiliating. But his statement on the subject fell on deaf ears in the upper chamber, and he was shouted down. In order to lend his argument demonstrative weight, he approached the chief minister for the navy and gave him a slap across the face. As a result, Almeida was sentenced to four months in jail, but he suceeded in his aim of having corporal punishment abolished.

The obelisk on the roundabout in front of the customs house in Faro was the first civic memorial in Portugal, erected on behalf of the Italian in homage to his friend. Over the years the monument sank into oblivion, and was reduced to the level of a Christmas tree, but it has since been rehabilitated in memory of Almeida and his sharp slap for justice.

Address Obelisco de Faro, Avenida da Republica, 8000 Faro | **Getting there** A 22, exit 13, Faro Centro, left at the train station to the marina, park at Hotel EVA by the bus station | **Tip** The Admiral Ortigão Maritime Museum is to be found on the marina. Next to the obelisk is the brewhouse-café Cervejaria Aliança, and the traditional coffee house Pastelaria Gardy is on Rua Santo António in the pedestrianised zone.

FARO

42_ The Old Harbour Inn
Senhor Joaquim and his cherubs

The old harbour inn, right next to the squat Porta Nova city gate, was once frequented by fishermen, sailors and wanton women, indulging in a few drinks and spending the summer nights in search of love. The bar in the middle and the beefy tiled stove in the kitchen of the former dive are still there, as if waiting for it all to get going again. The idea of opening a pub here in the former watch post next to the city gate, furnished as it would have been back then, is tempting, but this rendezvous for easy girls and tough guys has now been an antiques shop for more than four decades, and is stuffed full of religious artefacts and quirky works of art. On the bar itself stands a row of colourful flacons with ornate silver stoppers from a former perfume factory, full of musk, bitter orange, tobacco and vanilla scented oils. Classical music streams out through the open shop door into the square in front of the bishop's palace, and through the clouded glass panes in the door you can make out cherubs, madonnas, Baroque angels and gilded altarpieces all around the room.

The owner of this curious collection sits next to the radio. Senhor Joaquim was born in Porto, came to the Algarve 40 years ago, fell in love with it and stayed here. His interest in religious art has nothing to do with the church as an institution, he asserts, describing his eccentric passion for collecting as an addiction that has grown worse over the course of his life.

Most of the objects in his remarkable collection are from Portugal, others come from Italy, Austria and Germany; one piece is even from the old altar of Cologne cathedral. In the middle of the colourful *omnium-gatherum* is a Rococo piano. The keys work and it sounds harmonious, if perhaps a little out of tune. But who cares? Any kind of music, even slightly off-key, sounds wonderful in this extraordinary atmosphere.

Address Sitio das Antiguidades, Largo da Sé 22, 8000 Faro | **Getting there** A 22, exit 13, Faro Centro, Vila-a-Dentro, park at São Francisco car park; walk around the city wall to the gate of Portas do Mar (Porta Nova) | **Tip** Faro's old town, the Vila-a-Dentro, has enough to offer for a whole day's sightseeing – for example the Sé de Faro (cathedral) with its tower to climb, plus the treasury and bone chapel, or a visit to the Baroque city gate of Arco da Vila with its fascinating exhibition about the Portuguese guitar.

FARO

43_ The Old Power Station
Experience the sea with all your senses

In April 1910, the paraffin lamps that had previously been common in the city centre of Faro were replaced with electric lights. The first substation was built by a company from Lisbon in a building at the level crossing and ferry jetty at Portas do Mar. In the beginning the new service didn't always work the way it should – the street lamps flickered on, went out and then flickered again. This was acknowledged by the citizens of Faro with an ironic smile. 'Magellan is coming', was the cynical cry; everyone knew that the world-renowned Portuguese sailor and defector, sailing for the Spanish Crown, had never come back.

Fifty years later the electrical capacity was no longer sufficient to supply the city, so a new substation was built on the edge of town. The Faro fire brigade moved into the old building, before moving on to a more modern building in the 1990s. In 1997, after further conversion work, the Centro Ciência Viva do Algarve, an interactive science museum, took up residence in the former power station. Over the course of the years it has become established as a comprehensive centre for marine biology. 'Experiencing the sea with all the senses' is the motto of the museum, as is clear from the very beginning of the extensive displays.

You are taken through the geological genesis of the Algarve in 30 stages, coming across sea plants and marine life from tropical and Arctic waters in marine aquariums – just as thrilling as the Lisbon Oceanarium, though on a smaller scale. In the adjacent glasshouse you can get to know the flora of the Faro lagoon. Renewable energy is produced in the garden using tidal power and wind, and the potential for the creation of renewable energy off the coast is illustrated. The tour finishes on the roof. By prior arrangement you can come up here after dark and observe the night sky over the Algarve through a telescope.

Address Rua Comandante Francisco Manuel 41, 8000 Faro, www.ccvalg.pt | **Getting there** A 22, exit 13, Faro Centro, left towards the marina at the train station, park at Hotel EVA by the bus station | **Hours** Tue – Sat 10am – 6pm | **Tip** After a visit to the science centre, a boat trip through the coastal lagoon and nature reserve of Ria Formosa is an excellent idea. Various companies offer trips to the islands of Culatra, Farol, Ilha Deserta and Armona from the quay at the Portas do Mar city gate in Faro.

FARO

44__The Slaughterhouse by the Park
Paradise for peacocks and strollers

The Jardim da Alameda João de Deus was created at the end of the 19th century – an evergreen island in the heart of the city, with giant 100-year-old trees and blossoming flowerbeds, a pond, waterfall, fountains, mini-golf course and playground. Nowhere else in Europe will you find such a wealth of botanically diverse tree species on a one-square-kilometre open air plot. On a walk through the park, the noise of traffic shrinks to a far-off hum, the silhouette of the city disappears behind sweeping treetops, birds warble and peacocks eye visitors as they stroll by. It's a haven of peace and tranquility.

It was very different indeed when Faro's slaughterhouse was located right next to the park. This magnificent neo-Moorish building, with its imposing and opulent façade, was built in 1896, based on the Matadouro in Coimbra. The screams of the animals in the face of death were clearly audible in the park and further away – a rather horrifying experience for people out for a stroll. The slaughterhouse closed at the end of the 1970s, and since then the cries of frightened animals have ceased to be heard over the fence. The building then stood vacant for many years, until Faro council had it completely renovated.

Since 2001, the old slaughterhouse has been the new home of the António Ramos Rosa municipal library. Where once animals were butchered, books are now read and reading taught. Here both children and the elderly learn to read according to the Cartilha Maternal method, developed in 1876 by João de Deus, using pictures and speaking out loud as a group. Passing the frontage of the library's new home on Rua Pintor Carlos Porfírio, you can hardly imagine the fairytale *Arabian Nights* courtyard of the old building, never mind the macabre past behind it.

Address Jardim de Alameda João de Deus, Rua Carlos Porfírio, 8000 Faro | **Getting there** A 22, exit 13, Faro Centro, Vila-a-Dentro, from there follow the signs to Jardim da Alameda and Biblioteca Municipal | **Hours** Park: daily 7.30am – 8.30pm; Library: Tue – Fri 9.30am – 7.30pm, Sat & Mon 2 – 7.30pm | **Tip** Five minutes' drive from the library is Rua de Berlim and the Santo António church at the city's highest point – from there you have the best view over Faro to Estoi.

FERRAGUDO

45 — The Mandarin's Grave
The final resting place of a restless man

The Castelo de São João on Praia Grande in Ferragudo looks like an enchanted castle, with its terracotta façade, playful towers and arched windows. The former fortress, which has been converted into a private home, seems to have popped right out of a children's book, especially when viewed from the other side of the river in Portimão. Its site was originally chosen because of the range of cannons, and together with the Fortaleza de Santa Catarina, on the promontory of Praia da Rocha on the opposite side of the river, it watched over the shipping coming in and out of Portimão.

Decommissioned at the start of the 20th century, like all the fortresses on the Algarve coast, the guard fort in Ferragudo lay abandoned for several decades, until it was bought by Dr Joaquim José Coelho de Carvalho, the Portuguese ex-consul, ex-rector of the University of Coimbra, ex-diplomat and ex-lawyer. Coelho was a humanist. He didn't like the political developments in his country under Salazar at all, as they went against his principles. Whenever the opportunity arose, Coelho would proclaim his opinions against the dictatorial establishment in fervent speech and subtle words. As rector of the faculty in Coimbra he quickly fell from grace with his superiors due to his rebellious attitude, and he was retired early. Shortly afterwards his political poems, strongly influenced by his poetic role model Charles Baudelaire, were censored. He was strongly advised that he would be better off writing romantic poetry.

Weary from tilting at windmills for so long, Coelho withdrew to his fairytale castle in Ferragudo. Here the poet was better known among the people as the Portuguese mandarin. As a consul he had spent several years in the Portuguese embassy in Shanghai, and he spoke fluent Mandarin. The restless political poet found his final resting place in the cemetery of Ferragudo.

Address Cemitério Ferragudo, Rua Luís de Camões, 8400 Ferragudo | **Getting there** A 22, exit 5, Portimão, N 125 towards Lagoa, exit Ferragudo, further towards Carvoeiro, turn right at Praia Grande, park, follow the sign for Cemitério; the mandarin's grave is on the right, next to the main gate | **Tip** On the way to Carvoeiro is the Praia do Molhe vantage point, with stairs leading down to the pier. The next turn-off leads to the lighthouse at Ponta do Altar. From here you can get to the trendy beach of Praia dos Caneiros and one of the best fish restaurants in the region, Rei das Praias.

FERRAGUDO

46 The Scout Memorial
Scouts take their pledge by the anchor

You will often see girls and boys in scout uniforms around Ferragudo, especially at the weekend. They meet at the scout clubhouse, and might be found on the beach clearing up rubbish or taking part in group activities. In summer the *escuteiros* go sailing and learn important lessons about the sea, the moon and the tides while having fun on the water. The scouts from Ferragudo are members of Group 413 of the Corpo Nacional de Escutas, the only maritime scouting organisation from a total of 34 scout groups in the Algarve. This means that the members take on maritime responsibilities in addition to their usual scouting duties.

Like all their fellow scouts, the new members in Ferragudo, after passing the admission test, commit themselves to the Scout Promise and thereby pledge to act for the well-being of the group, to be true to the Bible, and to love their neighbours as themselves. The Scout Promise ceremony takes place next to the anchor memorial, which was erected in front of the parish church in Ferragudo in honour of the father of scouting, Sir Robert Baden-Powell, who founded the movement in 1907.

The British lord only visited Portugal twice, but his pioneering spirit had reached Portugal long before. While the young First Portuguese Republic was learning how to deal with its new political freedom, creating its first social structures as well as having to build up a completely new, purely secular education system, there was a need for a fresh, modern ideal for the next generation and their upbringing. Baden-Powell's scouting method was the redemptive anchor, which symbolises the stability that scouts find in their group and which unites all scouts around the world. The anchor next to the memorial plaque in Ferragudo serves as a meeting place for the scout groups when they celebrate their patron saint, Saint George, every year in April.

Address Igreja Matriz, Rua da Igreja 10, 8400 Ferragudo | **Getting there** A 22, exit 5, Portimão, N 125 towards Lagoa, exit Ferragudo; park by the harbour in Ferragudo and climb the zigzag steps by the lifeboat house to the church | **Tip** In the sacristy of the parish church there is a collection of sacred works of art, including the Madonna Rosário, which served as a model for the Cross of Portugal in Silves (see ch. 102).

FÓIA

47 — The Spirulina Algae Farm
Spirulina pioneers on the summit

You can see the summit of Fóia in the Serra de Monchique from anywhere in the west of the Algarve. The Algarve's green lung watches over the edge of the world and protects the coast from icy northeast winds and below-freezing temperatures. The mountain breathes salty air from the ocean and stores mineral-rich water in reservoirs, which are hidden deep in the granite rock. On this healthy land, the ancient freshwater spirulina algae have been thriving for several years alongside plants from five different continents. Spirulina is one of the most mineral-rich plants on our planet. It was known to the Aztecs and exploited by them for its nutritional value. Today spirulina is used in the pharmaceuticals industry and marketed as a superfood.

The idea of cultivating spirulina in Monchique on the Fóia mountain was hatched by a Portuguese woman and a Frenchman, who came across the algae in their search for a sustainable agricultural business. However, from this brainwave to the first harvest Cristina and George had to go through an unforeseen bureaucratic obstacle-course before all of the concessions for their pioneering project were granted by the Ministry of Agriculture. There had been no previous concessions for the cultivation of spirulina in Portugal, so all the documents had to be redrafted before the farm could finally open. Spirulina propagates in fresh water. The microalgae require a constant temperature of no lower than 25 degrees Celsius to thrive, which is why the tanks are in a greenhouse.

The spinach-green algae mass floats on the surface of the water as a viscous pulp. The mash is regularly skimmed and the algae mass air-dried in a complex process before being carefully packaged and transported to health-food traders. Make an appointment and you can visit Cristina and George, find out everything about spirulina and try Cristina's vegan algae dip.

Address Estrada da Fóia, Belém, N 266-3, 8550 Monchique, +351 929 043 275, spirulina-da-serra.com | Getting there A 22, exit 5 towards Monchique, in Monchique follow the signs for Fóia, left and left again at the Algarve Hill Station sign; the farm is at the end of the access road | Tip A bit further uphill along the main road is the Fóia spring, with a fabulous view of the south coast. The strenuous eight-kilometre circular hiking route PR 3 MCQ Trilho da Fóia starts and ends at the summit of Fóia.

FUSETA

48 — The Petanca Court
Sporadic rendezvous for a game of pétanque

Everyday life on the lagoon peninsula of Fuseta plays out at the fishing port and in the cafés and pubs around it. The dunes around the town are undeveloped and stretch for as far as the eye can see. There are no hotel resorts to disturb the laid-back mood of the fishing village. The Fuseta campsite next to the harbour pier is right on the bank of the estuary, in front of the car park. Boats travel from the pier to the islands offshore. The residents of Fuseta have, from time immemorial, lived from fishing and nowadays there is also the tourist industry. But the rhythm of life with the sea as their workplace continues to follow the ebb and flow of the tide; everyday life takes place around the fishing port in the cafés and on the squares, everything is done at a measured pace.

Leisure time is brief for fishermen – they only really have time off on Sundays. On land they must take care of their equipment, keep their boats in good working order, refuel them, overhaul the engine. When they aren't working, the fishermen of Fuseta are very talkative, reaching fever pitch on the issue of fishing quotas. If you buy them a drink, you'll soon make the acquaintance of José or Manuel and will be invited to play *pétanque* ('feet fixed' bowling) in order to deepen the ties of friendship.

The game with the steel balls is called *petanca* in Portuguese and is played here every day at some point in the afternoon, right next to the fishing huts and the campsite. The Fuseta *petanca* court, under shady sycamores, is the ideal place to meet and get to know people, wherever they may come from. You can play one on one, in pairs or in a trio, the teams are mixed and a game costs you a round of drinks for everyone. Not everyone speaks the same language, but that doesn't matter. The steel balls speak for themselves, and the desire for companionship always wins through.

Address Rua General Humberto Delgado G, 8700 Fuseta | **Getting there** A 22, exit 14, Moncarapacho, N 125 towards Tavira, in Alfandanga take a right to Fuseta | **Tip** The Ecovia Litoral bicycle and hiking trail goes through Fuseta. It takes you right through the middle of the lagoon region to Olhão or to Tavira and is perfect for long walks.

GUERREIROS DO RIO

49 The River Fishing Museum
Village of river warriors and smugglers

Between Álamo and Laranjeiras is the hamlet of Guerreiros do Rio, which means 'river warriors'. This name was originally given to the fishermen who made their living here on the Guadiana river and then to their home at some time later. The fishermen always had to fight against the river's current between ebb and flow, ever anxious as they cast their nets and lines that their boats didn't capsize or drift off with the tide. In the winter the river warriors used to catch lamprey. That was when the eel-like fish were nice and fat as they swam upstream to spawn, and they fetched good money at market. The fishermen had to beware of their bloodsucking jaws, as well as of the guns of the border guards on the opposite bank of the river in Spain, who might react nervously if a fishing boat from Portugal approached their side of the river.

The sustained military presence during the dictatorships in Portugal and Spain affected people on both sides of the river. But no one really wanted to cross over into Franco's Spain from Salazar's Portugal, except smugglers. The *contrabandistas* traded anything that they could make hard cash from or swap for other stolen goods. Before 1974, the smuggling of cured ham contributed massively to understanding between the nations on both banks.

The smugglers were also known as river warriors, and most of them were fishermen anyway. They fought every day for their livelihood, both against the current and against the risk of being caught red-handed on the 'green' border and being shot. The history of the fishermen and the smugglers, and the dangers they exposed themselves to, lives on in the ethnographic museum in Guerreiros do Rio. There are still river warriors here. Their fishing huts are on the jetty, but now they fish from their motorboats for pleasure.

Address Museu do Rio, Guerreiros do Rio, 8970 Alcoutim | **Getting there** A 22, exit 18, N 122 towards Beja, right in Odeleite towards Foz de Odeleite, from there follow the Guadiana north towards Alcoutim | **Hours** Tue–Sat: Oct–Mar 9am–1pm & 2–5pm, Apr–Sept 10am–1pm & 2–6.30pm; admission ticket valid for all attractions in the district of Alcoutim | **Tip** The riverside road continues on to Alcoutim. There is a marble sculpture on the jetty in memory of the smuggling era. From here you can take river cruises upstream to Mértola and downstream to Vila Real de Santo António.

LAGOA

50 The Fado Bar
A young girl on the path to becoming a fado diva

Even her name makes her sound like a star. She is Luana Velasquez, at just 12 years of age already one of fado's most promising voices. For Luana, singing is the elixir of life. 'A day without singing is a day without love,' she declares, wise beyond her tender years. Luana has sung since she could walk, she sings because music moves her, because everything she feels must somehow get out, as the young girl explains softly. Luana rarely speaks softly, and when she does you know how seriously she means what she says. Otherwise she speaks as she sings: with the whole of her body. She performs as if she has never done anything else in her life, and, just like her role models, the fado divas Mariza and Ana Moura, she strikes a pose as soon as she steps on stage. Her young yet powerful alto voice sounds alternately romantic, sad, angry and euphoric.

Luana sings fado songs by well-known and lesser-known *fadistas*, and she sings every one so convincingly, it is as if she herself had experienced the love, the death, the hope and the despair, the longing and the disappointment and all the other feelings she interprets. In order to understand fado, you need to understand other people, explains Luana. The young girl has already successfully demonstrated her distinctive vocal talent in several talent competitions, as well as the Portuguese version of *The Voice*.

Luana performs in the Algarve with local fado greats, and is herself already a real local heroine. Her parents support her and her singing talent, and have even opened a fado club in Lagoa, where, as in the fado bars in Lisbon, *caldo verde* and grilled *chouriço* sausage are served on fado nights. Of course, Luana sometimes sings here too, but only at weekends – after all, she has to go back to school on Mondays. On other days of the week, Luana's mother serves up regional food, daily specials, snacks and sweets.

Address Snackbar Nova Paragem do Onda de Fado, Rua da Liberdade 41, 8400 Lagoa | **Getting there** A 22, exit 5, Lagoa-south, third exit at the roundabout towards Centro; the snack bar is on the right-hand side of the main road | **Tip** A walk through Lagoa leads you to the city park, and further on through the pedestrian zone to the antique market hall and the Baroque parish church. Exhibitions and concerts regularly take place in the Convento de São José.

LAGOA

51 The Quinta dos Vales Vineyard
Where the customers create their own cuvées

The Quinta dos Vales vineyard near Estômbar has long been of interest to wine connoisseurs. For over 10 years the German Karl Heinz Stock, recently in partnership with his son Michael, has striven to make high-quality wines here and to establish a national and international market for them – and with great success. When no one on the national wine podium believed that Algarve wine could pick up international prizes, Karl Heinz Stock proved to the Portuguese confederate that the climatic and geological conditions on the Algarve create an optimum setting for the cultivation of robust vines, which produce full-bodied grapes for premium wines.

A decade later, the vineyard can now look back on a considerable series of own-label wines. Future vintages lie dormant in Canadian oak barrels in the cellar vaults of the *adega*, while upstairs new wine is maturing in stainless-steel tanks. A new addition to the range is so-called orange wine, made from white grapes with the pips, stems and skin retained. In this way the fruit ferments naturally with the juice, and the wine takes on a delicate orange-coloured nuance. Father and son are once again starting a new trend in the Portuguese winemaking scene, after first going against expert opinion to create a sparkling wine, and then successfully cultivating Alvarinho vines for Vinho Verde on their estate.

Their most recent project is running bottle-blending workshops, where the participants learn what wine blending means and how it works, and create their own personal *cuvées*. Longer-term barrel-blending courses are also available. In the future, Quinta dos Vales hopes to lease out plots with vines on the estate, so that anyone who dreams of becoming a winemaker can first try out viticulture on a small scale.

Address Quinta dos Vales, Sitio dos Vales, 8400 Lagoa-Estômbar, www.quintadosvales.eu | **Getting there** A 22, exit 6, N 124 towards Lagoa-south, first exit on the first roundabout, turn right after the level crossing and follow the signs for Quinta dos Vales | **Hours** Mon–Sat, tours and wine tasting by arrangement | **Tip** Very close to the vineyard is a sanctuary for donkeys, horses and other animals. Visitors and donations are welcome.

52 The Red Boulevard
Strolling along silent asphalt

As the first photos of the newly designed city centre of Lagoa appeared on social media, a regular tirade of comments broke out. Favourable responses to the fresh city image were counteracted by cynical mockery of the colour choice, and comparisons were made with Red Square in Moscow. The brick-red colour of the streets was discussed for weeks on end, and Lagoa was at the mercy of national public opinion for days, even appearing as a story on the eight o'clock news. It had long been agreed at the city hall that the road surface throughout the city centre was in urgent need of renewal. When work began, the old town was closed off for months, traffic was diverted and there was general congestion. This coincided with severe hold-ups for bypass traffic at both ends of Lagoa, which was also being diverted because the main through road was closed at the time due to roadworks.

Now all the roads and roundabouts are finished, traffic flows freely, and the jams that recurred daily during the summer at the two main junctions no longer happen. You can pass through Lagoa quickly, in whichever direction. And the red zone in the centre is certainly eye-catching. Because of the colour, the narrow road through the old quarter is clearer, and the parking spaces are better marked and easier to recognise. In the past, people parked higgledy-piggledy around the market hall, and a cacophony of car horns would often be heard when there was a hold-up.

Now the traffic rolls over the low-noise asphalt of the city centre quietly – the clatter of tyres over the old cobblestones is no more. A stroll through the red zone will take you to pleasant cafés and pretty boutiques, to the market hall with its butchers, fishmongers and florists, to various banks and the pedestrian zone. No one jokes about Lagoa's 'Red Square' any more; on the contrary, Lagoa is now proud of it.

Address Rua Coronel Figueiredo, 8400 Lagoa | **Getting there** A 22, exit 6 Lagoa-north, through the arched tunnel by the monastery, left at the next junction on to Rua Coronel Figueiredo | **Tip** The Baroque church is a short walk away from the red zone. There is a war memorial in the park in front of it in commemoration of soldiers from Lagoa who lost their lives during the colonial wars in Africa, in the former Portuguese colonies of Angola, Mozambique and Guinea-Bissau.

53 — The São José Convent
The secret of Ó

The old town of Lagoa begins at the arched gateway by the former Convento de São José, with its 18th-century chapel of Saint Joseph. For more than 100 years this convent offered poor women without property a roof over their heads and the opportunity to enter the mendicant order of the barefoot Carmelites, or to work as a lay sister. The nuns slept in small cells with windows opening to an enclosed atrium. They worked in the monastery garden and took in vulnerable women, children and orphans. At the 'door for the poor', in what is now the reception room of the former abbey, a wooden hatch may attract your attention. The hatch's past is just as dark and gloomy as it appears.

This was the so-called baby hatch. Here women could, anonymously, leave newborn babies from unwanted pregnancies. The nuns in the monastery looked after the child until he or she was old enough to work as an agricultural labourer for a fee paid to the order. A single lady from Portimão was responsible for arranging such work in the farmers' fields in the area. Sometimes childless couples also contacted her, and adoption deals were struck. Ironically this middle-woman in the trade of children, who was herself childless, was known by the code name of Senhora da Ó, in reference to the Portuguese cult of Our Lady of Hope.

The Dominican Order took over the monastery in the middle of the 19th century and established a college for girls. After secularisation at the start of the 20th century, the college closed and stood vacant for many decades, until the Lagoa city council renovated the building, which was reopened in 1997 as the city's cultural centre. A journal was found among Ó's papers in which the child trader had kept an account of her business. How many of the 600 permanently transferred children on the list came from the convent of the barefoot Carmelites remains Ó's secret.

Address Convento de São José, Rua Joaquim Eugenio Judíce, 8400 Lagoa | **Getting there** A 22, exit 6, exit Lagoa north, the road from the motorway leads to the arched gateway at the monastery; turn right there and park | **Hours** Tue–Fri 9.30am–12.30pm & 2.30–5pm | **Tip** Just around the corner from the monastery is Lagoa's 'red zone' with a market, boutiques and cafés.

54_ The Chapel of St Anthony
José Saramago and the people

The world-famous Portuguese author José Saramago was an expert at seeing through hierarchies, in particular the officially invisible entanglements between the government and the Catholic Church. The church is a very important theme in his literary oeuvre. The Nobel Prize winner generally represented the clergy, and its influence on the people and history of his country, in a poetically satirical way; sometimes they were cynically parodied, sometimes treated fancifully. Nonetheless, church buildings and their individual stories asserted a fascinating power of attraction on Saramago, and so one day he went off on a journey to the most interesting churches in his home country, which he wrote about in his enchanting book *Journey to Portugal*.

On his travels he talked to farmers, innkeepers and priests, fishermen, market traders and mothers, and he reflects on these encounters on the road in the form of a diary. His journey ended in the ethnographic museum in Lagos on the Algarve. Saramago wanted his trip to culminate with the ecstatic self-indulgence of Portuguese *talha dourada* – highly ornate gilded woodcarving used for the decoration of altars and other church furniture. In the chapel of St Anthony, which forms part of the museum, he stumbled upon an orgy of this flamboyant art form. The chapel is crammed with cherubs, angels and ornamentation, all covered in gold.

When he asked the curator of the museum the name of the artist who painted the ceiling fresco, Saramago received only a shrug of the shoulders in reply. But to his question as to who produced the fish traps made of willow branches, the fine lace and all the other hand-worked everyday utensils in the lovingly arranged museum displays, the curator answered reverently, 'The people.' Saramago breathed a sigh of relief. His journey had ended well – he had rediscovered his people.

Address Museu Municipal Dr José Formosinho, Rua General Alberto da Silveira, 8600 Lagos, +351 282762301 | **Getting there** A 22, exit 2, N 125 Lagos Centro; park in the car park by the river, cross the square in front of the church of Santa Maria and follow the alleyway by the pharmacy to the church of Santo António | **Hours** Tue–Sun 10am–1pm & 2–6pm | **Tip** On the left-hand side at the entrance to the pedestrian zone is the souvenir shop Mar d'Estorias, in the former church of Espirito Santo. Here you can enjoy breakfast and a view over the roofs of the city on the rooftop terrace.

LAGOS

55 The Church of Santa Maria
Here lies Henry the Navigator

Equipped with a wealth of castles – at Tomar, Silves and Castro Marim – Henry the Navigator, royal prince and Grand Master of the Portuguese Military Order of Christ, had access to hefty initial capital for his project to find a sea route to India. However, the actual cost of the expeditions ran well beyond the original estimates. Although the Portuguese crown earned a lot in taxes from maritime trade, this income wasn't enough to absorb the enormous expenses. Then Henry's vision was thwarted at Cape Bojador, in what is today southern Morocco, because the traditional sailing ships could not tack against the wind. The project stagnated and the prince's world fell apart. With maniacal zeal he urged his shipbuilders to construct a new type of ship with a moveable sail on the bow and the stern, something that was leaner, taller and more manoeuvrable. This prompted the development of the new Portuguese caravel, but the enforced delay almost bankrupted Henry. Gil Eanes from Lagos was the first explorer to conquer the notorious cape and then land on the 'gold coast' of what is today Nigeria. The discovery of diamonds and gold there, together with the start of the African slave trade, saved Henry's ambitious project of exploration, and his power was consolidated.

Only death was not negotiable. The initiator of the Age of Discovery died in 1460 in Lagos, and found his resting place there in the old church of Santa Maria in the parish of that name. It was destroyed during the earthquake of 1755, and a new church was built on the site of the former slave market. After the earthquake, the bones of the great prince were reburied at the abbey of Mosteiro da Batalha near Leiria. A bronze plaque in the square of Santa Maria da Graça commemorates the penultimate eternal resting place of the greatest Portuguese navigator of all time – who only ever went to sea twice.

Address Largo de Santa Maria da Graça, 8600 Lagos | **Getting there** A 22, exit 2, N 125 Lagos towards Centro; park in the car park on the river, cross the square in front of the new church towards the hospital and take the second street on the right | **Tip** Further along the street is a small fort with a military museum, by the old gate to the city. This is where the pilgrims' trail to the lighthouse at Ponta da Piedade begins, passing 14 altar niches with picture tiles which represent the Stations of the Cross. The trail ends at the fifteenth altar niche on the lighthouse.

LAGOS

56 — The Havaneza Café
Meeting place for Masonic conspiracy

The first official Freemasonry lodge in Portugal was founded in 1802, although there were already Masonic brotherhoods in the country before that time. It was instigated by a German aristocrat of the house of Schaumburg-Lippe, who was an army commander based in Lagos. The discussions about a fairer social system in Europe that he provoked in the officers' mess fell on receptive ears, and his invitation to become politically active quickly found followers in all strata of society. The German nobleman couldn't have chosen a better moment for his thought-provoking words. After the great earthquake of 1755, the middle classes and the intellectual elite in Portugal were becoming ever more vociferous against the power of the clergy, and there was readiness for the coming struggle to change the balance of power between the crown, the church and the people. Their joint revolutionary protests created a stir through all of Europe and were soon emulated in other countries.

From Lagos, Freemasonry spread through the whole of Portugal, and by the beginning of the 19th century there were almost 200 lodges around the country, whose Grand Masters were all linked with one another. *Maçons* worked their way into influential positions everywhere. Their aim was to topple the monarchy and to create a new political basis for democratic social structures. Their vision was realised on 5 October, 1910, though it foundered 17 years later due to irreconcilable internal conflicts of interest.

During the subsequent dictatorship, Freemasonry continued in secret, despite being banned. The lodge in Lagos has remained an international association since its creation. Its meeting place was at the Havaneza café on Gil Eanes square in the old town. Whether Freemasons still operate here is unclear, but the cocktails and snacks are delicious, and the clientele a nice mix.

Address Café Havaneza, Rua Marreiros Netto 37, 8600 Lagos | **Getting there** A 22, exit 2, Lagos Centro; park at the car park by the river, go past the town hall to Gil Eanes square, turn left at the clothes shop and then right again into Rua Marreiros Netto | **Tip** Past the war memorial on Gil Eanes square is the São Sebastião church with its skeleton chapel, which is only open during services. Behind the church is the Institute for Maritime Science. From here a bridge leads on to the roof of the market hall, which has a café with a view over the harbour and bay of Lagos to Alvor.

LAGOS

57 — The Putting Garden
Playing mini-golf on the roof

The old town of Lagos is enclosed by a sturdy wall with bastions that once protected its citizens from Corsican pirates. If you go on a sightseeing flight over the city you'll be able to make out its complete course; otherwise, a walk through the park gives you the best impression of its scale. In the past you would have reached Lagos, coming from Sagres, through the Porta Poente west gate by the former drill ground, and from there gone further into the city and to the harbour. There is a covered car park next to the city gate. A real surprise awaits visitors on its roof: a large roof garden with artificial grass and the Pro Putting Garden mini-golf course. The course is just like a regular golf course, with fairways, ponds and bunkers, flanked by bushes and flowers.

In between the miniature fairways are life-size sculptures in bold colours, decorating the mini-golf garden like an open-air gallery. Several voluptuous and exuberant naked ladies dance on tiptoes, alongside a bull, an elephant and a spitting frog. The delightful garden environment, with its view over the roofs of Lagos' old town, makes the putting course exceptionally attractive. In the shadow of the old fortress, families and groups of friends indulge in the game of skill, knocking the little white ball around the course on warm summer evenings and at weekends. But even for seasoned golfers, the course, with its twists and turns, presents a real challenge in practising the great art of putting.

There is an 18-hole putting green for adults, plus a second 9-hole course designed specifically for children, and both offer a whole lot of playing and fun. This is a great place to relax after a walk around the historic parts of the city or a visit to the museum. And, by the way, parking your car underneath, just five minutes' walk from the city centre, costs only 80 cents an hour.

Address Rua José Afonso 23, 8600 Lagos, www.proputtinggarden.com | **Getting there** A 22, exit 1, Lagos, take third exit on the third roundabout, towards the city centre, then left into the underground car park before the west gate | **Hours** Daily 10am – 10pm | **Tip** The alleyway behind the city gate leads to the Jardim de Júdice Cabral, a park with an open-air theatre, urban vegetable garden and youth centre. The city park stretches in both directions further out along the city wall; to the north there is an open-air fitness park and a drive-in cinema.

LAGOS

58 The Riverside Car Park
The harbour foundation stone is in the basement

Lagos harbour has moved three times. The location of the earliest harbour was only verified when an underground car park was built on the river promenade, and a harbour wall more than 10 metres high was exposed. Several massive sandstone blocks now two stories underground attest to the beginnings of the first fortified harbour in Lagos. This masonry, overgrown with moss and weeds, is almost 3,000 years old. The harbour quay was created by Phoenician seafarers, who conducted a bustling trade with the Celtiberians who lived here. The Phoenicians were followed by the Romans, who extended the existing harbour down to the beach of Praia Dona Ana, where its remains can be found.

But the Lagos harbour first became really important with the arrival of Henry the Navigator, who chose the fishing port as the start and end point of his expeditions, expanding the harbour basin and building a shipyard. During the Age of Discovery he instigated, money flowed steadily into the city and Lagos grew into a prosperous port for world trade. Historians refer to the Portuguese expansion into new worlds as the beginning of capitalism. The year 1444 is significant as it saw the start of the slave trade, when the first Africans disembarked in Lagos and were publicly auctioned in the market place. This business was to continue until 1758, when the slave trade was banned by the Marquês de Pombal.

Alongside a selection of archaeological finds that document the age of the harbour are human skeletons of African origin, probably those of slaves who had died in the bowels of the caravels during the crossing, and were thrown overboard upon arrival in Lagos. These were also found during the excavation work for the construction of the underground car park. This gruesome legacy is integrated into an interactive exhibition about the slave trade, in the building that was once called Casa India.

Address Garagem de Estacionamento, Avenida dos Descobrimentos, 8600 Lagos | Getting there A 22, exit 2, N 125, Lagos Centro, behind the courthouse and to the right is the entrance to the car park | Tip From the new church of Santa Maria you can walk to the city wall and the Forte da Bandeira citadel. A statue of the explorer Gil Eanes stands by the wall, and opposite is São Gonçalo, the patron saint of Lagos.

LAGOS

59 The Terminus
Slowing right down by train

Having just clattered across the railway bridge over the Arade river and seen from behind the ruins of one of Portimão's former canning factories, you travel on through the Alvor lagoon towards Lagos. The little train rolls through the Praia do Vale da Lama, a secret kitesurfing El Dorado, past the 18-hole golf course of Palmares, right by the sea with a view of the tongue of rock called Ponta da Piedade. The long waves of the Atlantic roar in, breaking with a fizz on the fine sandy beach, which is completely deserted in the winter and dappled in the bright colours of parasols in the summer. The train, decorated with graffiti, slows down, then eases into the terminus station of Lagos and stops at one of the two platforms.

Lagos' new train station is ultramodern, a glass box, with the floor, walls and front façade constructed using railway sleepers. You will recognise the old station, opposite the new one, as the Art Nouveau building with Portuguese faience and wrought-iron lanterns. Travelling through the Algarve by train means travelling at a measured pace. The route runs in a zigzag course from Vila Real de Santo António, all the way in the east, to Lagos in the far west. Travelling in a compartment shared with schoolchildren, commuters and holidaymakers, a train journey across the Algarve will offer you a variety of impressions that you wouldn't normally experience otherwise.

The railway lines of Linea de Comboio do Algarve and the fast train line to Lisbon meet in a village called Tunes. Here you can change for the train to Faro, or take the fast train to Lisbon. A trip from Lagos to Vila Real de Santo António takes two and a half hours including changes. The stations in Tavira, Olhão, Faro and Portimão are all pleasantly close to the town centres – ideal for a hop-on hop-off tour by slow train through the Algarve. Lagos is the last stop.

Address Estação de Comboio, Estrada de São Roque, 8600 Lagos | **Getting there** A 22, exit 2, Lagos Centro, at the first roundabout drive towards Portimão, at the Rotary roundabout keep right, then follow the signs to Marina de Lagos and Estação de Comboio | **Tip** If you follow the road along the beach you will reach the ruins of Forte da Meia Praia. Right at the end of the bay is the beach of Praia do Vale da Lama, where nudists and kite surfers meet.

LOULÉ

60__The da Graça Monastery
No admission for demons

The imposing arched gateway at Largo da Graça is a quite extraordinary sight. It's as if someone had just stripped it out of a wall and placed it here. The archway, originally the entrance to the church of Convento da Graça, is a stone picture book, decorated with mysterious symbols, figures and gargoyles. The convent, now completely destroyed, once served the Templars and later the Military Order of Christ as a hideout and meeting place, during the period of evangelisation of the defeated Moors. Today the gate, which now stands alone, leads to the ruins of the monastery beyond.

Stepping through the archway is like taking a spiritual step through a time portal, into an epoch in which faith and superstition dominated intellectual thought. Three mysterious symbols, chiselled into the stone, welcome those who pass through it with a message. There is a well-proportioned face with an olive branch as a symbol of peace, and a stone heart, out of which a flame flickers, as a symbol of charity. The third symbol, resplendent at the apex of the portal to the former monastery church, is a pentagon. In the religious mythology of the early Middle Ages, its five corners symbolised the five stigmata of Jesus Christ on the cross. For the Knights Templar, the mystical pentagon was a sign of truth, and they used this and other symbols to communicate encrypted messages. A rough interpretation of the message around the doorway could read: 'He who enters a house of God should do so with peaceful intent, out of charity and honesty.' According to folklore, the pentagon protects the church and its believers from demons, black magic and the devil.

The Inquisition categorised the pentagon, always previously interpreted as positive in spirit, as a symbol of black magic and of heretical exorcism. From that time onwards it was rigorously forbidden by the Catholic Church.

Address Porta do Convento, Travessa da Graça 3–5, 8100 Loulé | **Getting there** A 22, exit 13, N 125-1 Loulé, turn right at the junction (traffic lights) and follow the signs for the hospital; the gate stands on the Largo Tenente Mendes Cabeçadas | **Tip** Around 10 minutes' walk away at Rua Gil Vicente 14 is Loulé's museum devoted to dried fruit and nuts, where you can find out everything there is to know about the processing of figs, almonds and carob, and the history of the monastery bakery.

LOULÉ

61 The Lieutenant's Square
Mistake of a revolutionary

The life of José Mendes Cabeçadas, the former lieutenant from Loulé, was more swayed by the political events at the beginning of the last century than that of any other well-known person in Portugal. Graduating with distinction from the Marine Academy in Lisbon, he took command of the warship *Adamastor* right at the beginning of his career. Things couldn't have gone any better, he must have thought triumphantly, hoping that the cover he had been preparing for years wouldn't be rumbled.

As a staunch Republican, he was living a double life that involved danger at every turn. Cabeçadas knew that the day that would decide Portugal's future was edging ever closer. The coup against the monarchy had been prepared down to the smallest detail, and he already knew his mission. Early on the morning of 5 October, 1910, he gave orders to his crew, who were completely taken by surprise, to fire on the Palácio das Necessidades, the royal residence on the banks of the Tagus in Lisbon. The blast of the cannons was the signal for the rebels to strike. The revolt succeeded, the royalists put down their weapons, Portugal was declared a republic, and Mendes Cabeçadas went down in history.

During the political turmoil in the 17 years that followed the proclamation of the republic, the former revolutionary turned fickle, fighting against his convictions in the military revolt of 1926 – *for* the dictatorship. Once he realised what he had done it was too late – Salazar had seized power. The officer paid a high price for his mistake. To escape the charge of traitor, he renounced what he had done, earning himself the nickname of 'marionette' among his comrades. The assassination attempt on Salazar that he arranged in 1946 failed, but restored his reputation. Cabeçadas then disappeared into the underground, and continued to fight against the dictatorship for the rest of his life.

Address Largo Tenente Mendes Cabeçadas, 8100 Loulé | **Getting there** A 22, exit 13, Loulé, turn right at the junction (traffic lights) and follow the signs to the hospital | **Tip** Ten minutes' drive south of Loulé is Almancil and the Baroque church of São Lourenço, which is completely lined with original *azulejo* tiles from the 18th century.

LOULÉ

62__ The Piedade Hill
Puffing and panting for the matriarch

The main traffic arteries from Almancil and Boliqueime meet at the N 270 roundabout in Loulé. In the middle of the traffic island is an abstract sculptural installation. At first glance you may only see perforated metal, but on further inspection the spaces grow into figures. Then you can make out two men, their hands gripping the bars of a litter resting on their shoulders, on which a woman is enthroned with a child resting on her lap. The female figure represents the city's matriarch, Mãe Soberana.

What at first appears to be an abstract design cut into steel is in fact a homage to Loulé's *Homens do Andor*. These are eight upstanding men who carry a litter bearing the image of Our Holy Mother of Piety on their shoulders through the streets of Loulé every Easter, at the head of the Easter procession. Spread across their eight pairs of shoulders are 360 kilograms. It all begins on Easter Sunday at the Church of Piety on the Cerro da Piedade, where the procession down to the Church of St Francis begins. Two weeks later, on Divine Mercy Sunday, the *Homens do Andor* carry their matriarch back up to her church on the hill.

The Mãe Soberana processional ceremony has been a tradition for 500 years, and is the largest pilgrimage ceremony in Portugal south of Fátima. Tens of thousands of pilgrims follow the ceremonial march, and a deafening clapping of hands accompanies the eight litter bearers as they run past the cordon of people lining the steep path up the hill, panting loudly with the matriarch on their shoulders. The louder they are cheered on, the quicker they run. This requires a great deal of fitness and enormous willpower.

The artist Miguel Cheta has managed to precisely represent the immense will of the bearers in his steel creation. Their power lives in the empty space of the sculpture – you can't see it, but you can hear it whenever the wind blows.

Address Rua da Nossa Senhora da Piedade, 8100 Loulé | **Getting there** A 22, exit 12, M 396 towards Loulé, then to the N 270 roundabout | **Tip** You can either ascend the hill of mercy on foot, like the *Homens do Andor*, or approach its west side by car. The old pilgrimage church Nossa Senhora da Piedade is next to the modern domed church.

LOULÉ

63 The Poets' Café
People's poet António Aleixo and his quatrains

The well-known Portuguese literary hero António Aleixo was semi-literate as a child – he could read but not write. Born in Vila Real de Santo António, he moved with his family to Loulé, where he helped his father in his weaving workshop instead of going to school. The fateful day of 5 October, 1910 made a man out of the boy. Aleixo listened with fascination to the grand speeches about liberty, equality and fraternity on the day that the republic was proclaimed. He knew then that he wanted to become a poet, and read everything about humanism that he could get his hands on in the library. It was there that he met the teacher Joaquim Magelhães, who went on to teach the inquisitive boy to write by means of an unusual method. He first had the knowledge-hungry lad compose his own verses in four-line format, and then dictated them back to him in the correct written form.

Aleixo stayed true to this simple quatrain format, and his mentor helped him and his poetry to their first publication. The debut volume of his four-line verses was sold out in next to no time. Aleixo's calm, socially critical and simultaneously romantic poetry is infused with gentle irony, and it immediately found a large fan base. His popularity as a poet of the people catapulted Aleixo into the ranks of the most widely read poets in Portugal. People could understand him – craftsmen, traders and labourers identified with his poetry, as he wrote about them and their thoughts.

His personal career, from illiterate to nationally recognised poet, elevated Aleixo as a role model for social advancement. He became friends with the world-famous Portuguese poet Miguel Torga from the Minho area in north Portugal – both wrote in the language of the people. Aleixo now sits in sculptural form at a table in front of the Café Calçinha, where he sat so often in life, ready to scribble down the next stanza.

Address Café Calçinha, Praça da Republica, 8100 Loulé | **Getting there** A 22, exit 13, N 125-1 Loulé, left at the junction (traffic lights) to the roundabout, third exit towards Portimão and then look for a parking space; the café is on the left-hand side | **Tip** Right next to the café is the chapel of Nossa Senhora da Conçeição, a gem of Baroque architecture. Its nave is completely clad in Portuguese *azulejo* decoration.

MALHÃO

64_ The Buddhist Stupa
A sacred place on the Serra do Mú

The winding country road from Benafim to Malhão twists and turns up the Pé de Coelho mountain. The name means 'rabbit's foot' – the peak of the mountain has a bulge on it like a paw, on which the stump of a former windmill still stands. The vegetation on the mountainside is sparse. Puny strawberry trees and crooked cork oaks cling defiantly to the precipitous terrain. On the pass, the Mira Mar café invites you in to take a rest. From here you can walk straight on to Malhão, the only slate village in the Algarve. Squat houses made of slate flank the narrow village streets. Most of them have no windows and only open on to the world through colourful wooden doors with large keyholes. The one-way street leads through Malhão and back on to the main road towards Almodôvar.

On the other side of the street, opposite the café, a track forks off and ends up at the rabbit's paw. A circular herb garden marks the highest point on the mountain. Where once a second windmill stood, there is now a four-metre-high granite monument, surrounded by clumps of rosemary and lavender. This curiously shaped pillar is a stupa shrine in honour of the Buddha. The first stupa to be built in Portugal, it has been here since 2012. 'Those in search of meaning will find enlightenment here,' is the motto of the Tibetan religious community who live on the estate near the stupa.

The community runs a retreat centre for meditation, yoga and esoteric workshops here. From the stupa shrine, your gaze may wander over the Serra do Mú mountain range, far into the interior of the country and Alentejo, and to the east all the way to the wind turbines along the Spanish-Portuguese border. It is a sublimely beautiful place to meditate. The inhabitants of Malhão have got used to the community and their customs, including the chanting of mantras, and they now live in peaceful harmony.

Address Stupa-Associação para a Paz no Mundo, Moinho do Malhão, 8100 Salir, stupapaznomundo.org | **Getting there** A 2 towards Lisbon, exit S. B. de Messines, N 124 to Benafim, left to Sobradinho, right to Malhão | **Tip** The tranquil small town of Almodôvar in Alentejo, with all its attractions, is a 20-minute drive away. Almodôvar gives you a taste of Alentejo's everyday culture, which provides a noticeable contrast to life on the Algarve.

MARMELETE

65 The Santinha
A village learns to learn

The 'road to beautiful views' leads all the way to Marmelete from the granite quarry in Nave near Monchique. As it snakes along the Fóia mountain, eucalyptuses line the edge of the road like a guard of honour. Fern and bracken shine bright green under the canopy of silvery-grey leaves. Lagos, Portimão and Ferragudo, the Arade river and the Alvor lagoon lie spread out along the coast. The mammoth Algarve Motorsports Park comes into view in the midst of the seclusion of the Serra. Half a kilometre from the mountain village of Marmelete you reach a picnic area, next to which the Madonna of Safe Journeys greets those driving past. She stands in a niche painted light blue and white, and is better known as the Santinha.

The niche, built in the form of a star beam, was created according to a design by a teacher called Maria Guilhermina from Marmelete. This teacher was a real local heroine, who felt that her job was a calling. Driven by her passion, she campaigned for the universal right to education in the remote rural area. This was before education was compulsory in Portugal, when the law stipulated only four years of schooling in the village. For over 40 years, Maria Guilhermina taught the children of the village in the morning, officially and paid; then in the afternoon, unofficially and unpaid, she taught adults reading and writing.

Her pupils liked to learn. Through her commitment, the ambitious teacher lowered the rate of illiteracy in the district of Monchique, imparting to parents the principle that education is a human right, and thus creating a positive attitude towards compulsory schooling. The Ministry of Culture praised the teacher posthumously as a leading figure in the fight against educational poverty. Marmelete immortalised the resolute teacher by naming a square after her. And Maria Guilhermina left her home village the Santinha.

Address N 267, 8550 Marmelete | **Getting there** A 22, exit 5, towards Monchique, in Nave turn left at the quarry towards Aljezur; Santinha is right at the entrance to the village | **Tip** The circular hiking trail PR 6 MCQ begins at the parish church, leads through the village and continues out through the surrounding country to the Miradouro dos Picos viewpoint. In the Casa de Medronho museum in Marmelete you can find out how the legendary strawberry-tree fruit brandy Medronho is made.

66 — The Tollhouse-Madhouse
The king's extra-extra fig tax

The extraordinary feat of 18th-century engineering that is the Águas Livres aqueduct in Lisbon was a very costly project, funded by the introduction of a special sales tax, especially on the trade and export of olive oil and wine. However, even these new tax revenues were not sufficient to rebuild the country's ruined infrastructure after the earthquake of 1755. So the king, Dom José I, increased the rate of tax and decreed a new, additional charge – the fig tax. The fraternity of fig farmers groaned heavily, as figs were particularly popular as a dried fruit for export. The fig business was at least as lucrative as olive oil production, and it had previously been tax-free, but on the other hand, it was extremely labour intensive. Before the sensitive fruits could be properly dried and traded, they first had to be carefully picked by hand, one by one. Around a third of the crop was immediately discarded because it was either too small or overripe.

After the introduction of the new tax, it was the fig producers of the Algarve in particular who had to cough up, and they were forced to pay an especially high levy for their fruit. Rumours of nepotism and the personal enrichment of the tax collectors began to circle. From then on any dubious business in the Algarve has been jokingly named after the place in which the tollhouse for the 'extra-extra tax' on figs stood – an inconspicuous little village with the unpronounceable name of Mexilhoeira de Carregação.

It's a real tongue twister. Colloquially, the tollhouse was known as the madhouse, where the tax pirates stuffed their purses full, 'Mexilhoeira-style'. The customs office for the extra-extra fig tax of Mexilhoeira de Carregação was right next to the jetty for the ferry to Portimão. The building is still standing, and currently awaiting a new function – or the wrecking ball.

Address Rua Patrício Júdice 49, 8400 Mexilhoeira de Carregação | **Getting there** A 22, exit 6, N 125 towards Lagoa south, then Portimão, take the next exit, Parchal, turn right at the first roundabout to Mexilhoeira de Carregação and park at the harbour; the former tollhouse is on the river bank | **Tip** A short walk upstream are the saltworks and the tidal mill, under the steel-cable bridge. A little further on is the Ibn'Ammar grotto (see ch. 37).

MEXILHOEIRA GRANDE

67 — Algarve Motorsports Park
Motorsport fun to watch and join in with

After a record-breaking seven-month construction period, the Algarve's international motorsports park opened in November 2008. Since then, the four-and-a-half-kilometre-long race track in the middle of nowhere, north of Mexilhoeira Grande at the foot of the Serra de Monchique mountain range, has been a fixture in the international motorsport scene. For its opening ceremony it staged the final round of the World Superbike Championship. This baptism of fire ran smoothly and attracted tens of thousands of spectators to the circuit's very first race day. The futuristic-looking stands in racing red seat a total of 80,000 spectators, and offer excellent views of the demanding circuit, with its treacherous chicanes.

The project was seen as forward looking for the region, and was a real coup for the mayor of the district in office at the time. On the other hand, the noise pollution created by the park has caused great resentment among locals, and the destruction of habitat for wild animals in this otherwise uninhabited area has led to noisy protests among environmentalists. Despite all the resistance, the race track at the south-western end of Europe has now established itself on the international motorsport calendar and attracts a completely new set of visitors to the Algarve, with motorsport activities such as test drives, Superbike championships, motor races and classic car festivals.

The two-lane feeder road from the A 22 motorway leads directly to the park, and it's tempting to really put your foot down. But you'd be much better keeping to the speed limit, and then getting your kicks speeding around an actual racetrack in a racing car like a real pro. In the Kartódromo next door, everything is slightly smaller is scale, with one and a half kilometres and 17 turns waiting to be torn up in high-speed go-karts. Great fun for anyone with a need for speed.

Address Autódromo Internacional do Algarve, Sítio do Escampadinho, 8500 Mexilhoeira Grande, +351 282 405 650, www.autodromodoalgarve.com | **Getting there** A 22, exit 3, Autódromo Algarve | **Tip** During popular race events, you will come across lots of VIPs from the international motorsport scene in the bar of the Racing Hotel next to the track.

MEXILHOEIRA GRANDE

68 The Parish Church
A generous count and his fear of purgatory

The overpowering fear of purgatory of a local nobleman, Conde Castelo Branco Vila Nova de Portimão, is the reason for the existence of Mexilhoeira Grande's own parish church. The count hoped for forgiveness in return for this offering – he was more generally known as a *bon viveur* rather than a god-fearing churchgoer. And if general opinion is to be believed, the wastrel aristocrat did not change his lifestyle despite building the church.

For example, on Easter Sunday, for the amusement of his guests, he had sparsely dressed dark-skinned slaves perform local folk dances on the square in front of the church, rewarding them with raw meat. Furthermore, the village pastor also joined in the party, feasting at the opulent table that was set up in the church square especially for the spectacle. That both the count and the pastor went to confession and begged for forgiveness after the feast and dancing goes without saying.

The patron of the church also paid for the interior decoration, and had himself immortalised with his family coat of arms chiselled into the stone of the arch over the high altar. Peter and Paul keep vigil next to it, while the Virgin Mary kneels in the left side altar, ready for ascension; in the next altar, purgatory is ablaze. Both paintings are bordered by richly carved and gilded wooden frames.

Heaven only knows whether the count's generous whim ultimately saved him from purgatory. In any event, it was none other than the master of gilt woodcarving in the Algarve, Custódio Mezquita, who gave these two artworks their elaborate decoration and lustre. The technique known as *talha dourada* was used from the late Middle Ages until the Baroque period to make altars all around the country shine with gold. The second-largest treasure of this technique in Portugal is hidden in the Church of St Anthony in Lagos, and is Mezquita's masterpiece.

Address Igreja Matriz, Rua da Igreja, 8500 Mexilhoeira Grande | **Getting there** A 22, exit 4, Mexilhoeira Grande, then follow the one-way street through the village to the car park by the cemetery next to the church | **Tip** On the other side of the main road is Mexilhoeira Grande's railway station. This is the starting point of the eight-kilometre circular hiking trail PTM PR 1 Rocha Delicada.

MONCARAPACHO

69 __ Cerro da Cabeça
A hike on the trail of Atlantis

Moncarapacho is east of Faro, at the foot of a solitary mountain called Cerro da Cabeça. The mountain is a geological curiosity, its inside riddled with holes like a Swiss cheese. Sinkhole grottoes up to 100 metres deep open up like funnels under the bizarrely folded limestone rock on the surface, and in several places the mountain is completely hollowed out. The entry points are mostly so small that they're easily overlooked. It's a paradise for bats, who hide in the caves during the day and come fluttering out to hunt at night.

According to a local legend, Arraúl, the twentieth son of Hercules, wanted to build a second Atlantis here in the rocky tunnel labyrinth inside the mountain. One day, so the story goes, Arraúl disappeared without trace into the underground passages, never to emerge again. The sinkholes are still being explored and may yet be developed for tourism. The circular trail over Cerro da Cabeça leads, overground, past the traces of the mythical second Atlantis, up to the summit and back, with the Ria Formosa nature reserve and its island-lagoon world always in view. The hill and its rugged ancient rocks are home to a unique flora. Wild orchids, mastic trees, prickly pears, rock roses and fan palms fleck the barren landscape in green, white and orange, and line the hiking trail with their wild and rampant bushes. The trail is around seven kilometres long and can be distinguished by stones marked in yellow.

Near the summit you have to tread carefully between crumbling stone, deep crevices and jagged rocks. The assault on the summit will particularly please adventurous climbers – the final stretch to the trig marker at the peak can only be conquered on all fours. With a 270-degree panoramic view of Faro, Olhão and the 60-kilometre-long lagoon landscape towards the east, this is a wonderful place for a picnic.

Address Cerro da Cabeça, 8700 Moncarapacho | **Getting there** A 22, exit 15, first N 398 to Moncarapacho, then turn on to the M 1332 towards Este/Fuseta, left at the lights and left again straight away; turn left after two kilometres through a gateway and park (it isn't private property) | **Tip** The Monterosa olive estate not far from Moncarapacho produces gourmet olive oil. You can view the estate, the mill and the groves and book an olive oil tasting.

70 — The Catarina College
A holistic modern school for girls

The villa, painted pomegranate red and flanked by a garden, an orange plantation and cork trees, is known colloquially in Monchique as the castle. This spacious two-floor residence, with its many rooms and salons, is completely at odds with the village buildings all around it. The surrounding houses are limited in size to one or two rooms and are mostly single storey. The area below the castle is empty and littered with weeds, and serves residents as a parking space. This is where the Colégio Santa Catarina once stood.

The school for girls, initiated by a daughter of the 'castle' called Catarina Figueiredo, was a real revolution in 19th-century society – not only did the female pupils here become familiar with modern teaching methods, but they also practised manual duties. The nuns who taught them integrated their pupils into the everyday chores of the boarding school after normal lessons were done and taught them many practical skills for the future. Pupils helped in the vegetable garden, looked after small domestic animals, produced craftwork and needlework and worked in the workshop.

During the Salazar dictatorship after World War II, the college became unpopular. It was first converted into a mixed private school, before being integrated into Monchique's public education system after the Carnation Revolution. In the 1990s, a new school building was constructed in the village to replace the old one and the former college pulled down due to an acute danger of collapse.

However, in the 1960s its ideas came to be imitated at other schools in the Algarve, for example the Palácio de Casas Altas college in Faro. The college is open to girls as well as boys and is one of the best privately run educational institutions in the country. In this way the vision of Catarina Figueiredo from Monchique for more education and independence for girls lives on.

Address Rua do Castelo 16, 8550 Monchique | **Getting there** A 22, exit 5, towards Monchique, in the village continue in the direction of Fóia; park in the garage under the tourist office, from where it's a 10-minute walk to the castle | **Tip** The Caminho de Convento footpath leads past the castle and on to the remains of an old monastery. Explore the ruins at your own risk.

MONCHIQUE

71 — The Fire Station
Mountain village on the alert

The Monchique fire brigade's motto is 'to give life to save lives'. The volunteer association has already proven that it means precisely that on several occasions, most notably in 2003, in the severe forest fires that hit the area, which they were unable to quench. Helicopters from the Federal Border Police in Germany, together with teams from Portugal, Spain, France and Morocco, hurried to the aid of Monchique to fight against the inferno. Fire raged between Monchique and Aljezur and spread uncontrollably in all directions, guided by the continually changing wind.

A huge amount of water was used to fight the fire and endless tears flowed. Residents wept as they lost their property in the fierce blaze. The emergency teams cried through exhaustion and anger, because it seemed impossible to extinguish. After eight days and nights of non-stop engagement, the fire fighters finally managed to stop the blaze, but the aftermath was devastating. Cork growers had to write off their groves, Medronho farmers their strawberry trees, and the woodworkers of Monchique their supplies of wood for many years to follow. Cattle farmers lost their stock and nature lost its ecological balance.

With charred earth as far as the eye could see, the smell of burnt wood hung in the air for weeks on end. Monchique rolled up its sleeves, and everyone helped each other while working out what had to be done so that such a catastrophe wouldn't be repeated. First the forest was cleaned up, fire breaks were created and fire detectors were installed in the area. After that Monchique reorganised the fire brigade, equipping the station with new specialised vehicles and a helicopter landing pad, and finally the forest was replanted. The whole town pitched in. The message on the façade of the fire station reads 'Vida para Vida', reminding everyone of their collective promise.

Address Estrada de Sabóia, 8550 Monchique | **Getting there** A 22, exit 5, towards Monchique, through Monchique towards Lisbon; the fire station is on the left-hand side of the main road | **Tip** It's worth taking a trip to the Santa Clara dam, 35 kilometres away, at any time of year, but in summer be sure to pack your swimming things. One kilometre before the dam are the ruins of the Queen Dona Maria bridge, with a water lily pond and a population of turtles.

MONCHIQUE

72 — The Medronho Boutique
The firewater of Monchique

Medronho – poetically and melodiously pronounced 'med-ron-yo' – is a fruit brandy made from the berries of the so-called strawberry tree, *Arbutus unedo*. Its production is poetic too. The bitter-sweet, furry-skinned, spherical berries (which taste nothing like strawberries) turn orange-red and ripe from November on; they are then picked by hand and collected in large oak tubs. The berries are fermented until the alcohol in the mash reaches the required level for the distillation of the fine *aguardente*. The mash is heated and the rising vapour captured in a copper *alambique* distillation vessel and diverted through a narrow copper pipe. The vapour condenses in the pipe, and at the end pure medronho spirit trickles into a stainless-steel jug, where it rests for several weeks before being bottled. Locals call their unique spirit *mosquito* – it is known to have quite a bite, and the common practice is to drink a shot after a meal in order to aid digestion.

Strawberry tree berries flourish on tall evergreen bushes. The tree bears ripe fruit and blossom simultaneously in the winter. The white, bell-shaped flowers offer a rich source of nectar for bees, making for a exquisite bitter-sweet honey. The firewater of Monchique has a real kick to it, and of course all the farmers still distil their own spirit according to ancient family recipes in a barn behind the house.

There are, however, many strict rules governing its production for commercial trade. In order to share the bureaucratic burden, 52 producers have come together to form the Apagarbe distillers fraternity. They also have their own medronho boutique, Loja do Mel e do Medronho, where the medronho farmers take turns behind the counter and offer samples of their fruit brandy, along with honey, jams and preserves, as well as the drink Melosa, made by blending strawberry tree liquor with cinnamon and honey.

Address Loja do Mel e do Medronho, Rua Eng. Duarte Pacheco 18, 8550 Monchique |
Getting there A 22, exit 5, towards Monchique, drive into the village, park at the Lisbon / Portimão junction; the boutique is on the main square | **Hours** Daily 10am – 7pm | **Tip** A short distance on foot up the main road towards Fóia is the São Sebastião viewpoint with a car park and tourist office. A tour of the historic village centre begins here.

MONCHIQUE

73 __ Salvador's Workshop
Every wooden puzzle becomes a folding chair

Master carpenter Salvador is busy. He cuts ribs from the trunk of an alder, planes the edges and then sands the beautifully grained wood until the surface becomes silky smooth to the touch. On the workbench in front of him is an unmade jigsaw puzzle of wood for an item of furniture. The master pushes the pieces of wood back and forth contentedly, sticking one rib around and between the next and adjusting each piece until a structure emerges that looks like a pair of salad servers for a giant. Next the joiner fills out the open side with square slats, all of the same length, and fixes the joints with wood screws. Only then does he flip over the assembled puzzle, and now you can recognise a seat between two comfortable armrests.

The whole thing is a kind of stool. But not just any stool – this is a folding stool. The key to it is that you fold it up like a pair of scissors and put it somewhere out of the way, where it is always handy if you happen to be missing a chair. Being foldable makes the seat easy to transport, and it's also multifunctional. The *cadeira de tesoura* from Monchique is a unique local piece of joinery with a long tradition. The folding chair used to be called a *silla*, or saddle, and was a portable seat of power made of bone or slats of wood, with the seat itself made of a piece of animal hide.

Emperors such as the Roman caesars used this kind of portable stool: in those days it was customary that the ruler sat in an elevated position, with his subordinates on the floor at his feet. Sadly the folding chair has been in danger of dying out completely for many years. It is seen as a practical, but rather old-fashioned piece of furniture, rarely bought and then only by real fans. At present, Salvador is the only master in Monchique who still manufactures these stools by hand. Who will take over his workshop when he is gone remains uncertain.

Address Casa dos Arcos, Rua Estrada Velha 9, 8550 Monchique | Getting there A 22, exit 5, towards Monchique, follow the signs in Monchique to Portimão; the joinery workshop is on the left towards the edge of town | Hours Mon–Fri 10am–6pm | Tip On the way towards the coast you will pass the village of Caldas de Monchique. The romantic thermal spring spa invites you to take a walk to the springs and the chapel of Saint Teresa. The coffee tastes particularly good on the patio of the Albergaria do Lageado hotel.

MONTES DE ALVOR

74__ The Lawn Bowls Club
Bowling without skittles or pins

Montes de Alvor has one unique attraction, for sport fans in particular: the Alvor Lawn Bowls Club. Yes, that's lawn bowling in the Algarve! The playing surface, or bowling green, is a lawn with dense turf, similar to a golf putting green. The green measures 31 by 40 metres, and the grass is meticulously mown to a uniform length. It might seem that all is peaceful and easy-going among the young and old players at the Alvor Lawn Bowls Club. But this impression is deceptive.

What looks pretty easy is in fact rather difficult – and competitive. While in ten-pin bowling the ball is bowled after a run up, before rolling down a smooth polished parquet lane and crashing into a set of pins, in lawn bowling the irregularly spherical bowl is rolled along the grass towards a much smaller ball, or jack, at the other end of the green. The aim is to get as close as possible to the jack, while protecting the balls of your own team or clearing those of your opponents out of the way.

It's a game of skill, probably more than 7,000 years old, made famous by Sir Francis Drake – back in 1588, he insisted on finishing his game of bowls before he set sail to fight against the Spanish Armada. Concentration and staying power are essential. Etiquette must be followed, and rules observed. What at first seems elitist, is anything but. There is no dress code – you can play in comfortable clothes as a guest player, though club members wear matching shirts. The founder of the club, José Manuel Martins, wanted to establish lawn bowls played in the British way here in his homeland, and he opened this, the very first bowling green in Portugal, in 1995. His idea has yet to be emulated elsewhere in Portugal, so the sport and the club are still very much an insider tip in Montes de Alvor. The winner is the one closest to the little ball. You'll soon make friends in the clubhouse.

Address Urbanização de Santo António, Praçeta Júlio Amaro, 8500 Montes de Alvor, www.alvorlawnbowls.com | **Getting there** A 22, exit 4, towards Alvor, at the school in Montes de Alvor follow the signs left into the Santo António estate, turn right and right again | **Hours** Daily 10am–3pm, booking necessary | **Tip** Fans of boules play the Portuguese version, *petanca*, behind the sports hall, within walking distance of the Lawn Bowls Club, every afternoon. Guests are warmly welcomed and invited to take part. Reasonably priced coffee and refreshments are available in the clubhouse, with an extra portion of local colour thrown in.

MONTES DE ALVOR

75 — The Skydiving Centre
Meeting place for sky surfers

A sharp hiss cuts through the air, and your eyes search the skies in alarm, since that's where the noise is coming from. Then you spot black specks that rapidly grow bigger before unfolding into multi-coloured parachutes, with people hanging from each of them. Some laugh, others scream, some fall at breakneck speed, others float, until they all finally feel the solid ground beneath their feet again.

Skydiving is not for ditherers. It's an extreme sport for adrenalin junkies who find their ultimate kick in free fall. Men and women have fallen from the sky in Montes de Alvor for almost 20 years, and for many of them a lifelong dream is fulfilled at the skydiving school in Montes de Alvor. That leap into nothingness! The first time round you jump in tandem with an experienced skydiver, jumping from a plane at the lofty altitude of 3,000 metres for €250. The free fall lasts for only a few seconds – meanwhile your blood rushes to your ears, and there, where your stomach should be, is a hole. The euphoria bubbles over and vents itself in loud roars and screams.

Skydivers never forget their first jump, and no jump afterwards will ever feel as intense as the first. Skydivers from all around the world descend on Montes de Alvor. They come for a weekend, a day, just one jump, addicted to the complete freedom. First they tumble, then they float slowly, with a clear view of the mountain ranges of Monchique and Lagos over the Alvor lagoon, and back to the landing strip at the airfield.

It all began, amid a great deal of hype, on New Year's Eve of the new millennium, when skydivers jumped over Montes de Alvor for the very first time, and it eventually made history. Since then the skydiving school has grown from year to year, and Montes de Alvor is now one of the most popular skydiving centres in Europe. The school is open all year round.

Address Aeródromo Municipal de Portimão, 8500 Montes de Alvor, skydivealgarve.com | **Getting there** A 22, exit 4, towards Alvor, the airfield is on the right-hand side of the road after 2 kilometres | **Tip** Propeller planes fly several times a week from Portimão airport in Montes de Alvor to Lisbon. You can buy tickets on site or online. You can also book sightseeing flights over Montes de Alvor and the Algarve coast here, and if you want to try out parachuting, book a tandem jump.

ODECEIXE

76 __ The Beach Paradise
Sunbathing on one of Portugal's natural wonders

For summer holidaymakers, the Algarve is one big beach paradise. Over 200 sandy beaches are waiting to be explored between Vila Real de Santo António in the east and Sagres in the south west. They then continue past the cape, northwards via Carrapateira and Arrifana to Odeceixe and the so-called adventure cliffs in the Costa Vicentina nature reserve. Here, every holidaymaker can find their own personal favourite beach. The question of which beach is the most beautiful is superfluous – they are all beautiful. Nevertheless, the beach at Odeceixe is the official number one of the recently chosen Seven Natural Wonders of Portugal.

The bay, with its beach of fine, powdery sand, nestles in the lush, green, wide flood plain of Ribeira de Seixe, like an island between the rugged cliffs on the steep coast. Here, the Seixe divides the Algarve from its provincial neighbour – the Alentejo begins on the other bank, at the hamlet of Baiona. From its source in Monchique, the Seixe flows sedately towards its mouth, carrying more water in winter and less in summer. Where the river and the sea meet, the waves ripple and wild eddies are formed. The beach island and the river form a bow tied between sky and sea, a treasure for endemic plants and aquatic birds. White storks, peregrine falcons and choughs feel very much at home here. They nest in the nearby cliffs. At low tide they hunt crayfish, and when it rains they find worms. These splendid birds aren't easily disturbed by visitors, in fact they almost seem to enjoy being watched and photographed. This area therefore attracts flocks of birdwatchers.

The beach at Odeceixe has everything you need for a relaxing day by the sea. If you'd like to explore the area on foot, follow the Circuito de Praia de Odeceixe hiking trail. The next beach to the south, Praia de Adeagas, is a favourite spot for nudists.

Address Praia de Odeceixe, 8670 Odeceixe | **Getting there** A 22 to Bensafrim, N 120 via Aljezur in the direction of Lisbon to Odeceixe; at the mountain in Odeceixe follow the signs to Praia de Odeceixe | **Tip** The windmill in Odeceixe and the Ethnographic Museum in the local council offices, as well as the village itself, are all worth a visit.

ODELOUCA

77_Fonte Santa
Only a few know the way to the holy spring

The warm holy springs of Monchique are all in the middle of nowhere; only a handful of farmers know their exact location. One of those who did was known as the cunning Zé. He took adventurous tourists to see them on his donkey in exchange for hard currency. Whether it was Zé or the donkey who departed this life first no one knows for sure, but since then the area where hikers once refreshed themselves at the sulphate-rich springs has become overgrown. When the Odelouca dam was being built, the then mayor of Monchique immediately put a project on the table to develop the springs into a tourist attraction.

However, the project failed due to environmental concerns, and the way to the springs is still known only to insiders. It begins in front of the dam, at the sole signpost to Fonte Santa on the left side of the road, and then leads through a tunnel of trees. This outing is a wonderfully fragrant experience, especially in February, when nature explodes and blossoms, and mimosa, acacia and wild oleander speckle the forest with colour. You cross the Odelouca stream three times on the three-kilometre route to the springs. Watch out – after heavy rain the stream can swell to knee height or deeper. It should be waded across with trousers rolled up and waterproof footwear, and not barefoot.

After crossing the stream for the third time, the path splits, the right path turns half-left between two rocks and then continues uphill, hardly recognisable, over slate and downhill through a grove. It ends at the ruins of three houses with two holy warm springs. Nothing about the place is beautiful, and after rain the path can be quite muddy, but there is a footbath in the plunge pool, lined with clay bricks, and the experience of peace itself compensates for the lack of spa luxury. You're sure to be pleasantly revitalised for the walk back downhill to the car.

Address Fonte Santa Alferce, GPS coordinates: 37.297561, -8.494479 | **Getting there** A 22, exit 5, N 124 towards Monchique, in Porto de Lagos turn right towards Silves, after two kilometres go left towards Alferce, then after five kilometres right towards Baragem Odelouca. The wooden sign to Fonte Santa is on the left-hand side; take plenty of drinking water, provisions and wear suitable waterproof footwear. | **Tip** The Odelouca dam is the largest reservoir in the Algarve. It is at the end of the only access road, so you rarely see other people here and can enjoy the peace and the magnificent view.

OLHÃO

78 The João Lúcio Palace
The sad poet and his fairytale castle

At the campsite in Olhão is a pink fairytale castle. Its architect, João Lúcio Pereira, was a famous poet. He began his literary work at the age of 12 with lyrical verses, and later founded the journal *Echo of the Academy* at the University of Coimbra. During his studies in Coimbra he met the poet, philosopher and mystic Teixeira de Pascoaes, a staunch advocate of the Portuguese literary and aesthetic movement of *saudosismo* and the nostalgic messianic faith known as *Sebastianismo*. Completely captivated by this occultist world view, Lúcio joined a secret society, whose followers held clandestine meetings in the Quinta da Regaleira palace in Sintra, carrying out their sacrificial cult practices in the caves and grottoes of the Quinta park, which were designed to reflect their mystic ideology.

Obsessively fascinated by this enticing parallel world, Lúcio designed a villa with a similarly esoteric concept at the Quinta Marim in Olhão. The ground plan of the building represents the cross of the Knights Templar, with four three-storey towers oriented to the four cardinal points, and the three storeys of each tower symbolising birth, life and death. Four flights of steps lead to the palace, the design of each subtly allegorising the four elements of earth, air, water and fire. From a bird's-eye perspective you can make out a fish, a snake, a Portuguese guitar and a violin.

The palace served as a refuge for the poet. Here the ardent monarchist could give free rein to his lyrical torrents in the style of the great 16th-century master, Luis de Camões, considered Portugal's national poet. Yet despite his mystical inspiration, Lúcio was never able to breathe such humanistic depth into his life's work as his role model Camões. Lúcio died in 1918, shortly after the accidental death of his son. The museum displays items relating to his life and work.

Address Casa Museu João Lúcio, Parque Campismo e Caravanismo, 8700 Olhão | **Getting there** A 22, exit 15, towards Olhão, right at the roundabout, take the next road on the left towards the campsite and turn left before the railway embankment | **Hours** Mon – Fri 9am – 12.30pm & 2 – 5.30pm, guided tours by arrangement | **Tip** Beyond the railway embankment is the Parque Natural Ria Formosa. Among the sights of this huge park are the nature trail, visitor centre, Roman fish salt basin and tidal mill (see ch. 81).

OLHÃO

79_ The Ria Formosa Nature Reserve
A seaweed meadow for seahorses

Skipper João from Sabino Boat Tours has radiant sea-blue eyes that shine a little brighter as soon as he starts to talk about *his* Ria Formosa. The sea and the lagoon are his elements, they give him work and a livelihood. Up until a few years ago João worked as a mussel farmer, until he bravely took the initiative to set up his boat trip business.

He didn't want to zoom at high speed from island to island. Instead, João enables his guests to experience the marine ecology of his hometown quietly, discreetly, and in an environmentally friendly way, with biology lessons on board. On a relaxing boat trip through the enchanting lagoon world off Olhão, you explore one of the most fragile ecosystems in Europe. Twice a day the 60-square-kilometre nature reserve, classified as a protected maritime area since 1987, fills up with sea water and then empties again. Sandbanks, mussel farms and meadows of seaweed that are hidden under the water at high tide suddenly appear. The seaweed in the Ria Formosa converts carbon dioxide into oxygen by means of photosynthesis, and thus contributes to the generation of important organic matter for the biocosmos in the lagoon.

Off the island of Armona, João's guests can snorkel, and observe one of the largest seahorse colonies in the world in their seaweed meadow. On the way, João stops off at the oyster beds and shows you how to harvest oysters, razor clams and cockles. The trip continues through swamps near the shore, where flamingoes, egrets and spoonbills stalk around. On the way back the skipper does an extra lap through the basin of the fishing harbour, past the offshore trawlers and tuna catamarans. With João and his crew you experience a bespoke boat trip and a biology lesson, with lots of fun for the whole family.

Address Avenida 5 de Outubro, 8700 Olhão, +351 915 661 860, www.sabinoboattours.com | **Getting there** A 22, exit 15, towards Olhão, follow the signs towards Porto; park on the promenade. The Sabino Boat Tours information stand is next to the ticket booth on the ferry pier. | **Tip** On Saturdays a farmers' market and a market of bric-a-brac are held in front of, behind and next to Olhão's imposing market halls, in Parisian marché style.

OLHÃO

80__Santa Maria Lighthouse
222 steps to the best view of the coast

The Santa Maria beacon at Farol, part of the island of Culatra, fulfils all of the lighthouse clichés. Built in the middle of the sand, the tower has watched over the sky and ocean at Cape Santa Maria, the most southerly tip of continental Portugal since 1851.

Bright white, slender and round, the tower, packed in a corset of reinforced concrete, juts 50 metres up into the air, with a bright red lantern, glass dome and observation terrace at the top. The staircase inside the tower twists up in a spiral, winding like a snail shell, with 222 steps leading to the lantern. Only those with a head for heights should take to the observation platform, and even then the refreshing wind is sure to cause a rather queasy feeling in the stomach. The best way to enjoy the view is with your back to the wall. The view to the west extends to the sandstone coast of Quinta do Lago, to the east to the end of Ilha de Tavira, inland to the fishing town of Olhão and all around the lighthouse, over to the fishing village of Culatra at the other end of the island. In the middle of the island is a former Allied military airbase from World War II called Hangar.

The lighthouse keepers welcome visitors on Wednesdays between 2pm and 5pm, taking tours through the lighthouse and explaining technical details. You will find out how the rotational system and the lighting-up system works, all about the light signal itself and what the crystal prism is for. At the end of the tour you will have learned the rhythm of the pulsating light, that it is visible 46 kilometres away and that every lighthouse worldwide has its own distinctive signal.

You can reach Farol with the island ferry or a water taxi from Olhão; the trip takes 15 minutes. It's a good idea to extend your visit to the lighthouse into a relaxing day on the island with some beach time, a walk and lunch, or combine it with a boat trip.

Address Farol de Cabo de Santa Maria, Rua L. Galvão, Ilha de Farol, 8700 Olhão | **Getting there** A 22, exit 15, N 398 towards Olhão, right at the roundabout towards Faro, third exit at the next roundabout, right at the next roundabout, park on the left of the harbour basin; the jetty for the island ferry is straight on through the small park. Tickets available just before departure. | **Tip** It's a five-kilometre walk along the beach from Farol to the fishing harbour of Culatra, where you can catch the island ferry back to Olhão, with a stop off on the island of Armona. The timetable is displayed on the wall of the ticket booth in Olhão.

OLHÃO

81 The Tidal Mill
Bela Moura Floripes and her admirers

Her gaze is directed towards the sea, her eyes know of pain, her long hair flows down her back in waves and touches the ground like the hem of her dress. Floripes with the sad, yearning eyes was left alone after first her father, and then her beloved were lost at sea. The beautiful Moorish girl lived all on her own in her house at the tidal mill of Olhão. No one ever saw her leave the house during the day. Only under the cover of darkness did she go out to take care of her garden and her chickens – and of a fisherman, who turned up at the mill every night and found shelter in the barn. Every night, once he was asleep, Floripes brought the fisherman something to eat. If he cried in his sleep, she would wipe away the bad dreams from his brow with gentle kindness.

One day, at the market in Olhão, the fisherman met a young man and told him about Floripes and her kindness. The young man was desperate to see the beautiful Moorish girl and to court her, though his heart already belonged to another woman. The beautiful Floripes immediately saw through the young man's pretensions of love, sent him back to his betrothed and instead gave her heart to the fisherman, whom she sheltered and honoured to the end of her days.

Floripes is seen in Olhão as the guardian of love. A bronze statue of her stands on the Praça Patrão Joaquim Lopes, just across from the market halls, and serves couples as a romantic photo motif for selfie threesomes. Most of them don't know Floripes' story, but they want to be close to her anyway. Her house and the water mill can be reached on a walk along the banks of the lagoon, through the forest and Quinta de Marim park on the eastern edge of the city. This Moinho de Maré is one of only three tidal mills still in operation in Portugal. On the roof terrace you can enjoy a view of the island paradise world off the coast of Olhão.

Address Moinho de Maré, Ria Formosa Parque Natural Quinta Marim, 8700 Olhão | **Getting there** A 22, exit 15, towards Olhão, go right at the roundabout and left at the next road on to the Avenida de Parque Natural da Ria Formosa, go past the campsite, over the railway crossing to the bend, then left into the park | **Tip** The huge covered fish market at the docks of Olhão is a culinary must. Nowhere else on the Algarve will you come across such a huge variety of fish, shellfish and dried fish. Here you can buy *muxama* (salt-cured tuna) and, if you dare try it, dried octopus roe.

PADERNE

82 The Museum of *A Avezinha*
The four Marias and their newspaper

Behind the church in Paderne are the original editorial offices of the local Algarve newspaper *A Avezinha*, now a museum and a library. Four poets, who were known in the literary scene of 1920s' Algarve as the four Marias, founded the paper in 1921 as a fund-raising initiative, for revenue to support a friend who had gone blind. Their paper was full of poems and news from the surrounding area and conceived very much as light reading, spreading the news as if by the twittering of birds, as is implied by the name *A Avezinha*, which means 'little bird'.

The 'four Marias', who published under the pseudonyms of Madressilva (Honeysuckle), Violeta, Rosa and Hortênsia (Hydrangea), were joined in the course of time by four more writers, who took the names of Gardênia, Margaríta (Daisy), Orquídea (Orchid) and Camélia. The women all chose the names of flowers as pen names for their lyrical verse, and each had her own characteristic style. Orquídea, the eldest, was known in particular for her articles in biting, often ironic verse, that grappled quite critically with the political situation in the country. That was dangerous – the censors saw poetry in particular as a sharp literary weapon for spreading hidden conspiratorial messages. The paper was banned in 1936 for the possible dissemination of seditious messages.

In 1977, three years after the Carnation Revolution, *A Avezinha* returned to enrich the local press, revived by 'Madressilva' with Arménio Aleluia Martins as editor-in-chief, and it continued in circulation until 2014. Today Senhor Arménio still publishes local and sports news online, and looks after the museum as a volunteer. He speaks English and French, and tells the story of the four Marias and their 'little bird' on the guided tour through the former editorial offices and the museum.

Address Rua Miguel de Bombarda 67–69, 8200 Paderne, +351 289 367 673 | **Getting there** A 22, exit 9, IC 1 towards Lisbon, exit Tunes towards Paderne; in the village follow the signs to the church (Igréja) | **Tip** At the end of the street is the Casa Acordeão, a privately-run museum with over 3,000 exhibits relating to the accordion.

PENINA

83 — The Feather Cliffs
Picturesque trail in the Serra de Caldeirão

Curved like a bird's feather, the raised crest of the Rocha da Pena *cordillera* is on a 400-metre-high, rugged rock massif in the middle of the Serra de Caldeirão. The M 1094 country road goes from Benafim straight to the foot of the mountain, past the hamlet of Penina and on over a sand track to a handful of isolated farms. You can park next to the village well and refresh yourself in the only bar for miles, assuming that it's open. This is where the dramatic and picturesque LLE PR 18 Rocha da Pena hiking trail begins – a 6.5-kilometre circular route up to the crown and then back down again on the other side.

A refreshing wind whooshes through gorges and crevices, sometimes whispering quietly, sometimes howling loudly. In the early morning the mist kisses the dry loam and makes it damp like clay. Rays of sunlight break on the spider webs hanging between strawberry tree bushes and decorated with pearls of morning dew. The air smells of cistus and lavender. The ascent is strenuous, but completed after around two kilometres. Several wind turbines stand in a row on the mountain crest, inland in the direction of Alentejo. Their rotor blades use the alternating warm and cold blowing westerly winds that sweep powerfully over the summit from the Atlantic Ocean. The path continues on along the crown to the black and white striped summit pillar at the trigonometrical point, which is a short climb up. But the last push is worth it. From here you can see out over the whole of Serra de Caldeirão to the coast from Vilamoura to Albufeira.

The trail ends in the hamlet of Penina. With a bit of luck the local history museum there – the smallest on the Algarve – will be open, to offer insights into rural life in this isolated area. The museum is in a farmhouse that has been lovingly furnished by villagers in traditional style, with antique fixtures and fittings.

Address Rua de Rocha da Pena 601 Z, 8100 Salir | **Getting there** Drive in the direction of Lisbon; at the motorway junction A 22/A 2, exit S. B. de Messines, go towards Alte, and on to Benafim; from there in the direction of Almodôvar and after two kilometres right to Penina; Bar das Grutas is on Rua de Rocha da Pena | **Tip** The Rua Rocha da Pena continues as a track that takes you straight on back to the main road and the village of Salir. This is a fortified medieval stronghold with a museum, fortifications and historic village centre.

PORCHES

84_ The Algarve Potteries
Insider meeting place for music fans and expats

The district of Lagoa has a lot to show off – as well as its picture-postcard beaches and bays and finely blended wines, there is its local ceramic craftwork. From the preparation and mixing of the raw materials to the painting and glazing of colourful fruit bowls, everything happens under one roof in the traditional pottery workshops in Porches. Around half a dozen ceramic workshops and smaller potteries in Porches (*potarias* in Portuguese) are specialists in the production of ceramic tableware, flower vases, plant troughs, sculptures, tiles and wall decorations and offer their products, most of which are completely hand-crafted, in a large selection of diverse designs.

One of these potteries is Casa Algarve, housed inside a typical and historic Portuguese merchant's house. Here, fans of ceramics can browse in peace for the right present for friends and family or indeed for their own home. Each piece of ceramic purchased is carefully packed in bubble wrap and then in packing paper so that the fragile stoneware won't break in your suitcase on the flight home. This mansion on the outskirts of Porches is *the* address for hand-painted earthenware and exceptional decorative pieces.

To make customers and the inquisitive feel even more at home, there is a café on the premises. It has delicious daily specials, coffee and cake, as well as music at the weekend. Live music, from country to folk to jazz, is on offer on Fridays and Saturdays, and on Sunday afternoons there's an open jam session. Musicians of various nationalities and age groups meet here from around 4pm, bringing their instruments and of course their voices, and improvising off the cuff with charm and flair, for a real feel-good atmosphere. There'll be singing along, dancing and listening – everything that expats and locals could need to communicate through music.

Address Casa Algarve, N 125/299B, 8400 Porches, casaalgarve.wixsite.com | **Getting there** A 22, exit 7, N 125 towards Lagoa / Porches, left on the main road | **Tip** Anyone who loves messing about in the water can get their kicks at the Aqualand Algarve leisure park, ten minutes' drive away on the N 125, left just before Alcantarillha.

PORTIMÃO

85 _ The House of Fear
The long shadow of the secret police

Portugal is still centrally governed, so every communal issue lands in Lisbon. It can take quite some time for decisions to be made. But when certain things need to change quickly, Algarvians have always taken matters, as far as the law allows, into their own hands – and not only since the Carnation Revolution. This is something they are very proud of.

The rebellious nature of Algarvians is epitomised by rebel role models like Remexido from São Bartolomeu de Messines, the separatist leader and bank robber Palma Inácio from Tunes, and the instigator of the Olhão rebellion against Napoleon, for the recovery of the sovereignty of the Algarve. However, even the most defiant of rebels had to show respect for PIDE, the dreaded national security agency, or secret police. Their house of fear in Portimão is now a private residence, inconspicuous in a side street not far from the cemetery.

Agents of the PIDE secret police in Portimão also hired informants, and snooped around with painstaking precision for so-called politically conspiratorial subjects in the underground. The agents made continual attempts to unsettle the general public through machinations or with faked arrests, but they weren't very successful. Drunk fishermen and sailors regularly ended up in the drying-out cell of the House of Fear, arrested umpteen times for blaring out banned fado songs while under the influence, whereas those who pulled the strings in the separatist movement LUAR escaped PIDE's clutches.

On the day of the revolution, 25 April, 1974, most of the agents took off for fear of the public's anger, others were caught and some simply disappeared. When you pass by the former agency of the secret police today, you can think yourself lucky that the time of police informants and spies is over, and that for more than 40 years people here have once again been free to say what they think.

Address Rua dos Herois da Restauração 3, 8500 Portimão | **Getting there** A 22, exit 5, Portimão Centro, join the right lane, take the fifth exit at the roundabout, go on towards Bombeiros; take a U-turn at the next roundabout and park in the underground garage under the market hall. Walk along the first road to the left towards the city centre. | **Tip** The old town around Alameda square is only five minutes' walk away. The pedestrian zone leads to the millstone monument; the nearby Café Brasil serves excellent seafood.

PORTIMÃO

86 — The Junction of Freedom
Three streets tell the story of revolution

The three avenues of Avenida Zeca Afonso, Avenida Miguel Bombarda and Avenida 25 de Abril meet in the middle of the harbour city of Portimão. The names of these major streets symbolise the two great Portuguese revolutions of the last century, which led to the fall of the monarchy in 1910 and the overthrow of the dictatorship in 1974. One of these streets is named after the republican and parliamentarian Miguel Bombarda, who for many years supported the Charcoal Lodge, a militant offshoot of the Freemasons, in its scheme to overthrow the monarchy.

Zeca Afonso is the name of another. Everyone in Portugal has heard of Zeca. He was the legendary songwriter who composed music with messages to the underground during the dictatorship. At some point his musical encryption method was rumbled, and his songs were banned and censored. His most famous song, 'Grândola, Vila Morena', is about a village in Alentejo which, figuratively, is brown as the earth. It described the beginning of the Marxist-influenced movement in Portugal and the organised fight of the underground. Separatists used to hum the song as an identifying melody when they were secretly preparing for the planned revolution.

When 'Grândola, Vila Morena' was broadcast on the radio in the early hours of 25 April, 1974, the revolutionaries knew that the time had come, and they struck. The military coup against the dictatorship began at dawn on 25 April and ended that afternoon, with carnations for the soldiers as a symbol for the regained freedom. This is why 25 April, 1974 went down in European history as the Carnation Revolution.

The intersection of these three streets symbolises the three pillars of democracy: liberty, equality and fraternity. In the water park with keep-fit apparatus there, a portrait of Zeca Afonso is painted on the wall; next to it is the text of the Portuguese anthem of freedom.

Address Avenida Miguel Bombarda 11, 8500 Portimão | **Getting there** A 22 exit 5, Portimão Centro, turn left at the Continente supermarket into Avenida Miguel Bombarda, and go on to the junction at the police station | **Tip** The market hall with fish and vegetable stalls in Rua Albuquerque, 10 minutes' walk away, has 9,000 square metres of trading space, an underground car park and cafés, and is currently the most modern market hall in Portugal. It is open six days a week, mornings and afternoons.

PORTIMÃO

87 — The President's Office
Where the spirit of the city's father walks

A family tree in the foyer, made of finely sculpted bronze leaves, welcomes visitors to the birthplace museum of Manuel Teixeira Gomes. Leaf by leaf, it tracks the branches of the family of the father of Portimão city, right up to the present. Gomes' interest in politics was ignited on the day that the First Portuguese Republic was proclaimed. He was among those who stormed Portimão city hall, relieved the mayor of his office and shouted 'Viva a república!' from the windows. Thirteen years later, the people elected Gomes as their President of the Republic, and the following year he conferred municipal rights to the city of his birth.

Change was his watchword for Portimão, and it would appear that the citizens really took this to heart – it continues to change constantly. In no other city in the Algarve can you see so clearly the continual (and not always positive) transitions in the infrastructure over the past 60 years, and all within a small area. Gomes wanted to lead his country into a liberal future, but the highly conflicting interests of individual parties diverged much too strongly for them to be able to find common ground, and the lobbyists were extremely assiduous in trying to thwart the sociopolitical plans of their head of state. After countless resignations of presidents and prime ministers and all their respective cabinet reshuffles since 1910, the First Portuguese Republic was destined to fail.

Completely disillusioned, the penultimate President of the First Republic announced his resignation in 1925 and chose a life in exile in Oran in Algeria, where he wrote about his ideas for reform towards a fairer future, with social security for the working class. His private library and a collection of his writings, diaries and other documents can be found in the Casa Manuel Teixeira Gomes museum. Gomes' dream of a fairer future lives on here.

Address Rua Júdice Biker 1, 8500-701 Portimão | **Getting there** A 22, exit 5, Portimão Centro, park in the car park by the city hall | **Hours** Mon–Fri 10am–6pm | **Tip** The coffee house Arade, three doors down to the left from the museum, serves homemade Algarvian confectionery specialities and wafers filled with an egg-white whipped cream, a speciality from northern Portugal.

PORTIMÃO

88 — Quinta do Marisco
Scrabbling lobsters and lively lugworms

If you're after fresh seafood to feast on or lively lugworms to use as fishing bait, Senhora Odete's specialist shellfish shop Quinta do Marisco is the place to go. Here you will find local delicacies from the Atlantic shores, freshly collected and certified for sale. Pale pink-coloured, almost translucent coastal shrimps lie alongside shiny crimson Cardinal prawns from the Rio Guadiana estuary. Then there are whelks from Costa Vicentina, barnacles from Arrifana, cockles, razor clams, oysters and many others too numerous to list, harvested from the rocks and mudflats of the Ria Formosa lagoon in Olhão and the Ria de Alvor estuary at Alvor. The selection of crustaceans and molluscs varies according to the time of year and the protected seasons for shellfish.

Mussel farmers harvest their haul between the tides, before immediately handing it over to the local port authority. Here the catch is registered in their name and then transported in a so-called *purificadora*, where the shellfish take a bath in salt water and get a dose of UV light to filter out any impurities, so that they reach the shops cleaned and sterilised. In Senhora Odete's shop, the crabs, langoustines and lobsters crawl around in a 1,000-litre tank of seawater, from which they are fished out and individually selected for the customer. There are also finely-meshed baskets hanging in the tanks, full of lively lugworms squirming around. While one customer carefully selects the finest crustaceans and molluscs, another is buying lugworms in bulk.

Alongside fresh seafood, Senhora Odete also offers specialities like squid, scallops and deep-sea shrimps from the freezer. Local specialities like cured tuna, salt cod and gourmet tinned fish, as well as a choice selection of wines, round off the delicious range. Ready-to-serve steamed crustaceans are also available if ordered in advance.

Address Rua Professor Doutor Montalvão Marques, Bloco A – Loja A, Quinta da Malata, 8500 Portimão | **Getting there** A22, exit 5, towards Praia da Rocha, then to Zona Ribeirinha, third exit from the next roundabout, right at the next roundabout and straight on for 250 metres | **Tip** Walking straight on from Quinta do Marisco, you will reach the city hall in the 18th-century Palácio Bivar. This is where the pedestrian zone begins, leading to the main Alameda square with the Jesuit church Igréja do Colégio and the 550-year-old parish church Igréja Matriz.

PORTIMÃO

89 __ The Sardine Cannery
Tinned fish and its epicurean comeback

In the past the shrill howl of a siren would make the housewives of Portimão sit up and take notice, urging them off on their way to work in one of the city's 27 fish canning factories. But those days are gone. The sirens have fallen silent, the factories no longer exist. The timing of the siren would depend on when the fishing boats returned. The catch went directly from the boat into the factory, where the sardines were beheaded, cleaned and descaled. Sorted according to size and quality, the clean sardines then went up a floor to be tinned. Here the next brigade of workers would place each fish, individually and by hand, into tins on a conveyor belt.

The women on the conveyor belt would generally work for 10 hours or longer without a break, until all of the catch was cleared and all of the sardines had been sealed in their tins. Young mothers would take their babies with them to the factory, breastfeeding them from time to time, and then continuing with their work. The female factory workers' pay packet noticeably augmented the family income back then, especially in the 1960s, when a general economic recession created social poverty all over Portugal. From the 1970s onwards, the canneries all went out of business, one after the other, though the former factory women didn't stay unemployed for long – they found a new working future in the then nascent tourism industry.

The sculpture of three figures in coloured marble, on the roundabout by the job centre in Portimão, commemorates the hard-working women of the sardine factories and the economic importance of their role in the canning industry in Portimão. Gourmet tinned fish such as cod roe and sardine roe are currently experiencing a culinary renaissance. However, the canning is no longer done by hand, but instead by ingenious technical means, and sales are generated through creative marketing ideas.

Address Rua Dom Carlos I, 8500 Portimão | **Getting there** A 22, exit 5, Portimão Centro, after the tunnel merge on to the V6, take the third exit on the second roundabout, turn right at the lights into Rua Dom Carlos I | **Tip** The industrial museum in the former Feu cannery contributes to the commemoration of the local canning culture. It is two minutes' walk from the roundabout (entrance on the riverfront).

PORTIMÃO

90 — The Stone Tear

The Stone Age rock in the middle of the pavement

In the Pedra Mourinha industrial park, under the expansive canopy of a medlar tree in the middle of the pavement, is a large, almost tear-shaped lump of rock. The boulder is about four metres long, one metre tall and just as broad, and it is a geological witness to the history of our planet. The rock is from the early Stone Age, of a type that occurs in Monchique, but not on the coast. How the rock giant got from the mountains to Portimão has not yet been scientifically proven.

Its mysterious name 'the Moorish Stone' goes back to a traditional story about a Saracen princess, who lived with her family in a palace in the mountains of Monchique. When the impetuous girl with vivid blue eyes and coal-black hair grew up to be a woman, all the young men in the area fell in love with her. But the princess only had eyes for one and staunchly rejected all of the other suitors. Her father was a powerful vizier in the caliphate of Silves; he wanted to marry his daughter to a different man to ensure that she would be well taken care of. But love often pays no heed to wealth, and so the beautiful girl continued to meet in secret with her chosen one, who was no prince, but a kindhearted peasant boy. The couple managed to conceal their secret relationship for many months, until one day the two lovebirds were caught together. Blinded by rage, the father sent the unwanted suitor into the army, to battle against invading Crusaders at Portimão, where he ultimately died a hero's death.

When the princess found out that her beloved had been killed, she began to cry and didn't stop. Her tears flowed down from Monchique to Portimão, to the place where he lost his young life, and there they turned to stone. The boulder has been here ever since, according to local legend, and no one, not even with the help of a bulldozer, has ever managed to move it an inch.

Address Rua da Pedra 5–7, Pedra Mourinha, 8500 Portimão | **Getting there** A 22, exit 5, Portimão, past the Aqua shopping centre to the Maxmat roundabout, towards Praia da Rocha, turn right at the next roundabout into Rua da Pedra | **Tip** If you follow the main road further towards Praia da Rocha and Centro, you reach the Parque da Juventude with a garden area, duck pond, playground, picnic area, skateboard ramps and other open-air attractions.

PORTIMÃO

91__The University Cellar
Mystical water reservoir from the Arabian Nights

In the heart of the old town is the old fishing quarter of Barca, where all the alleyways are one-way streets and the narrow houses crowd together wall to wall. At the end of Rua Santa Isabel is the college ISMAT, which offers degree courses in law, architecture, psychology and business management.

The university institute is housed in a 19th-century mansion, and the canteen in the courtyard also functions as a public café. If you are lucky you can nab a bistro table in the sun on the patio and sit next to blossoming bougainvilleas, protected from the wind by a 1,000-year-old fragment of the city wall. Here you'll get a great meal at student prices. In the in-house library, row upon row of modern shelves stand under Gothic-style cross vaults, housing a remarkably large selection of literature on art and architecture.

A door in the middle of the yard leads to a staircase and this, in turn, takes you 14 metres down into the 1,000-year-old cellar under the university. The scent of damp earth rises up, and with every step down the air gets heavier, like in a tropical greenhouse. The last step ends on stone tiles, and you find yourself standing in the middle of a Moorish cistern with a domed ceiling, supported by six columns. The walls are plastered with clay and lime, the column pedestals decorated with sculptural work. The reservoir, which contains several cubic metres of water, probably belonged to a royal residence. The building structure is reminiscent of an antique hammam in old Constantinople. The cistern in Portimão is the only completely preserved legacy from the earlier Moorish city of Burtimûn, which was over 1,000 years old when it was destroyed in the earthquake of 1755, and now lies buried under today's houses. You can view this mystical place by prior arrangement with the university office. In the summer, concerts are sometimes held here.

Address Rua Doutor Estevão de Vasconcelos 33a, 8500 Portimão | **Getting there** A 22, exit 5, towards the train station, from there go on to the river and park at the bridge; on foot, turn right beyond the bridge through the yard of the Dona Barca restaurant, uphill to the ISMAT institute | **Hours** Campus and café Mon–Fri; book a visit to the cistern at info@ismat.pt | **Tip** The Dona Barca restaurant serves charcoal-grilled fish. At the weekend there is live accordion music and fado.

PRAIA DE ALEMÃO IN VAU

92 — The Soares Residence
Private refuge of the founding father of democracy

Behind high ivy-covered walls at Praia de Alemão is the former residence of Mário Soares. The founding father of resurrected Portuguese democracy used to spend his holidays here. Soares successfully led his country into the Third Republic after 25 April, 1974, confidently fending off all parliamentary adversaries.

His interest in politics was piqued at an early age – as a student he was already rebelling against the regime of Salazar, and with his eloquent and thoughtful nature he easily won followers who would oppose the dictatorship with him.

His name soon appeared at the top of the secret police blacklist. After repeated interrogations by agents of PIDE, the police for internal security, Soares saw that moving first his family and finally himself out of the country was the only possible course of action. In exile in France, Switzerland and Germany he looked for political allies to mobilise against the dictatorship, and in 1973 he founded Portugal's Socialist Party (PS) with the support of Willy Brandt.

When Soares heard 'Grândola, Vila Morena', the song that had been banned by the censors, on the radio the night before 25 April, 1974 – the signal for the start of the planned revolution – he immediately set off for home. He reached Lisbon from Paris three days after the coup of the Carnation Revolution, travelling in what later became known as the freedom train. He took the reins of the transitional government without hesitation and assumed his first political office as foreign minister. In his career as a statesman, Soares governed Portugal several times as prime minister and for two legislative periods as president.

Whenever he was able, he would withdraw to his villa on the Algarve. He died in 2017. Most of his essays on the theme of social policy, which have been translated into countless languages, were written here.

Address Praia de Alemáo in Vau, Urbanisação Vau da Rocha, 8500 Portimão | **Getting there** A 22 exit 5, Portimão, follow the signs to Praia da Rocha, at the roundabout in Rocha go right towards Alvor, at the roundabout with the bust of Miguel Bombarda drive back in the opposite direction and turn off to the cliffs on the first road on the right; the painted blue gate belongs to the Soares residence | **Tip** The clifftop hiking trail to Alvor begins here, past the cliff promontory of Ponta de João Arens with its mysterious Templar signpost (currently being renovated).

QUELFES

93 The Olhão Argonauts
David against Goliath

When Napoleon sent troops from Spain to Faro on 16 June, 1808, in order to deprive the Algarvians of their sovereignty by force, a group of rebellious fishermen from Olhão banded together and went into battle. They angrily tore the French flag from their Portuguese royal coat of arms, cursed the invaders, who had defiled and plundered their churches and mocked their faith, armed themselves with scythes, pitchforks and shotguns, and hatched a devilish plan.

They would obstruct the French armada's entry into the harbour at the estuary off the island of Farol, besiege the headquarters in Lethes palace in Faro, and then lie in wait for the advancing infantry on the Roman bridge in Quelfes, hidden in the reeds. Despite their lack of weapons, and although enormously outnumbered by the French, they managed, like David against Goliath, to come out on top, capturing the French commander General Maurin and proclaiming the restoration of the Algarve on 18 June, 1808.

Still in the first flush of victory, the rebel agitators boarded the one-mast sailing boat *Bom Sucesso* and set course for Brazil, to bring the happy message of the Algarvians' liberation struggle to their king Dom João VI, who was living in exile in Rio de Janeiro. The ship was caught up in a fierce storm, but the victorious rebels, equipped with a high measure both of trust in God and of navigational experience, reached Rio safe and sound. There they were greeted triumphantly, and were venerated and richly rewarded by the king for their heroic deeds.

The *Bom Sucesso* is docked in front of the market halls of Olhão in commemoration of the rebellion, and the rebels' Argonaut journey is immortalised in picture form in Olhão as a cobblestone mosaic, on the wall of the tunnel in Avenida Doutor Bernardino da Silva. A stone plaque on the bridge in Quelfes commemorates their important battle.

Address Ribeira de Marim, 8700 Quelfes, Olhão | **Getting there** A 22, exit 15, towards Olhão, exit Quelfes, turn left at the church in Quelfes and follow the road to the bridge | **Tip** In the old town of Olhão is the old fishing quarter of Barreta with its unique Moorish medina-style houses. In the west of the city is the José Arcánjo football stadium, the home of the only football club in Portugal to have been champions of the first, second and third leagues.

QUERENÇA

94__ The Museum of Water
The Portuguese donkey and the Arabian well

The square in front of the Baroque church in Querença buzzes with life. The year begins with a tribute to the patron saint of animals, and ends on Christmas Eve with a prerecorded cock-a-doodle-doo. In this small hamlet, off the beaten track on a hill in the mountains, elderly women make dolls out of left-over fabric, and men collect willow branches for basket weaving. Neighbours meet in the cafés to chat and eat Sunday lunch. They talk about the weather, the harvest, about recent births and deaths.

Very few here go down to the coast – it's only the young people who go to the beach. In the past, all the villagers would walk to the beach together once a year, on 29 August, for the washing and blessing of their animals. This annual bathing ritual still lives on, but today people drive down there, and there is no herding of cattle into the sea.

But the greatest wealth of the area is out of sight: there are huge aquifers under the ground, full of fresh water. Springs bubble up all around Querença, and in other places the groundwater is pumped up through deep wells. In the past, water was brought to the surface using bucket wheels with clay jugs attached to them. The water-raising device called the nora came to the Algarve with the Arabs.

The large wheel would be set into motion using a chain drive, and groundwater would be drawn up from a considerable depth. The water was first collected in basins and then fed on through a network of canals. To drive the wheel, a donkey fixed to a drawbar would walk in continuous circles, thus keeping the gear mechanism in motion. The exhibition in the Museu de Água water museum in Querença shows how it works. There are still a number of old nora well wheels in the area, most of them rusty and overgrown. Others are still being used, but these are now powered by electric pumps and no longer by donkey.

Address Museu de Água, Largo da Igreja Nossa Senhora da Anunciação, 8100-127 Querença | **Getting there** A 22, exit 12, towards Loulé and on towards Salir, to the Querença junction | **Hours** Mon–Fri 9am–1pm & 2–5pm | **Tip** The reception area in the museum also serves as the local tourist office. Here you can get information pamphlets about all the villages, hiking trails and nature parks in the area, and ask for the church to be unlocked for a visit.

RAPOSEIRA

95 — The Guadalupe Chapel
The Black Madonna of Raposeira

The Black Madonna of Guadalupe stands with the holy child on her arm on the plain, linen-covered altar. The wooden figure poses quite a riddle, since the Guadalupe cult arose in Spain, in Salado in the province of Cádiz, during the successful recapture of Andalusia with the active support from the Portuguese. The figure in the Ermida de Nossa Senhora de Guadalupe in Raposeira is more recent, and more of an artistic work than a sacred one. She is devoid of anything celestial. There is no brocade dress embroidered with sparkling gemstones adorning her body, no halo shining above her head.

The ancient pagan cult of the dark-skinned Madonna goes back all the way to the Visigoths' invasion of the Iberian peninsula. According to legend, the image of the 'guardian of the waters' was created by Saint Luke and later taken to Rome. Pope Gregory presented the Guadalupe Madonna to Bishop Isidore of Seville. At the beginning of the Moorish invasion in the 8th century, priests buried the figure at a farm near Salado for fear of desecration. After the aforementioned battle of Salado, a cowherd found the Black Madonna under a dead cow, but as he was about to eviscerate it, the cow jumped to its feet alive and kicking, and a vision of Our Lady of Guadalupe appeared.

Her appearance was interpreted both in Spain and in Portugal as a divine sign of victory for the Crusaders over the Moors. Thus the Guadalupe Madonna and her symbolic power reached Raposeira. The plain Romano-Gothic chapel is the oldest existing Christian building in the Algarve, and it served as a place for prayer for the Portuguese Order of Christ during the recapture of the Algarve. A century later, the Grand Master of the order, Henry the Navigator, visited the chapel and stayed nearby. An exhibition documents the course of the Portuguese Age of Discovery and the spice trade with India.

Address Ermida de Nossa Senhora de Guadalupe, N 125, 8650 Raposeira/Vila do Bispo | Getting there A 22, exit 1, towards Sagres; around 500 metres beyond the village of Figueira turn right to the chapel | Hours Mon–Sat 10am–1pm & 2–5pm | Tip The 'Rota do Infante' ticket, with special rates for all the sights of Vila do Bispo and Sagres, is available here. It includes the entrance fee to the Alcalar Stone Age site in Penina.

ROGIL

96 The Sweet Potato Restaurant

A potato with a place in every cooking pot

Peanuts thrive in Rogil. Muslim farmers actively developed the cultivation of the underground nut in the region and generally contributed to making the area arable with their agricultural knowledge. When the former Moorish kingdom of Al-Gharb became the Kingdom of the Algarve and the Portuguese sailed to new worlds, explorers brought unknown fruit and vegetables back with them from their daring expeditions to Africa, India, Indonesia, China, Japan and Brazil. These included hot peppers, teas, exotic fruit and a tuber from Brazil, the *batata doce* or sweet potato.

The slender, quaintly shaped tuber prospers extraordinarily well in Rogil and many farmers now grow them. They are nutritious, free of cholesterol and go with just about everything. Whether prepared with fish, meat or seafood, the sensory characteristics of the sweet potato marries with other ingredients to create completely new nuances of flavour on the tongue. And it absolutely comes into its own in confectionery, creating epicurean delights that will even please those who don't have a sweet tooth.

In the district of Aljezur, the sweet potato has grown into an agricultural ambassador for the region, and a culinary festival in its honour takes place every year at the end of November. In the market halls of Aljezur you can buy the usual variety, lyra, purple on the outside, orange-yellow inside, and another, smaller variety that is blue-red on the inside. They contain lots of vitamin C and are perfectly suited as food colourings. The restaurant Museu da Batata Doce in Rogil serves delicious cooked and baked treats made of and with sweet potato, as well as sweet potato beer and vodka, true to their slogan, 'Taste the best sweet potato in the world'. Cheers and enjoy your meal!

Address Museu da Batata Doce, Rua da Poente 6, 8670 Rogil | **Getting there** A 22 to Bensafrim, N 120 to Aljezur, on towards Lisbon, turn left on the far side of Rogil; the restaurant is immediately on the left | **Hours** Daily 7–2am | **Tip** The circular hiking trail Circuito de Amoreira, a section of the Grande Rota Vicentina, begins south of Rogil on Pedra da Mina. The six-kilometre walk with blue-green markings will take you to Amoreira beach in Aljezur, then along the cliffs and back past the Serrão campsite.

SAGRES

97_ The Electric Tuk-Tuk
Cruising the Cape of Sagres with zero horsepower

Rui Cruz and his electric tuk-tuk are more familiar to locals throughout Sagres than the postman. Every morning the former transfer chauffeur zooms silently and pollution-free back and forth through town, showing guests *his* Sagres. A tour of Sagres usually takes one hour – or maybe a bit longer, Rui winks. There will be stops for photos on the Ponta da Atalaia cliffs, at Mareta beach and at the memorial to Henry the Navigator, before you head off through the side streets, where Rui tells stories of the famous, infamous or just really nice people of the neighbourhood, towards 'whaling bay' and the fishing port of Baleeira, which takes its name from the Portuguese word for whale. Here among the fishermen his guests find out a lot about the art of fishing past and present, learning the difference between deep-sea and coastal fishing as well as various techniques such as longline, weir and net.

The second tour in his programme also begins at the tourist office on the main street and heads westward. After a detour to the mariners' fortress Fortaleza de Sagres and down to the beach of Praia de Tonel, Rui follows the country road westwards to the lighthouse. On request he will stop on the way at Forte Beliche and at a pottery. Once there, Rui explains all there is to know about the lighthouse and its importance to seafaring and aviation. There's time to take some photos and for a wander around the mobile market place before the rubber duck on the handlebar of the electric limousine tuk-tuk quacks energetically, to indicate it's time to go.

The electric-powered vehicle, which seats six guests in comfort and safely belted up, rolls back to Sagres at almost 60 kilometres an hour with zero horsepower. It's a leisurely tour around the cape of Sagres for all the senses, during which Rui will tell you lots of stories that you definitely won't read in a guidebook.

Address Meet at the Tourist Office, Rua Comte Matoso 75, 8650 Sagres; Rui Cruz, +351 914 011 230 | Getting there A 22, exit 1 Lagos, N 125 to Sagres, left at the roundabout, straight on at the next roundabout and park on the right at the tourist office | Tip A variety of boat trips leave from the fishing port of Sagres. At Sereia, the restaurant above the auction hall, you can eat fish fresh from the boats while watching the day's catch being auctioned through the panoramic windows.

SAGRES

98 The Pet Cemetery
The final resting place for dogs and cats

The Portuguese call the promontory of Sagres 'Holy Point'. This has to do with the mystery of St Vincent of Saragossa, after whom the nearby cape is named, and his incredible story. After his martyrdom at Valencia in Spain, the legend has it that his corpse, accompanied by two ravens, mysteriously came to Sagres, where it is said to have lain buried until the Christian reconquest of the area. But the magic of the place stretches even further back in time. In ancient manuscripts, scholars described this forbidding place with its giant sheer cliffs at the end of the world as a holy place for the worship of gods and dubbed it 'land of serpents'. The Celtiberians buried their dead here and erected menhirs, Romans worshipped their sun god Sol. Christians and Muslims both once flocked to the promontory: for one group it was the end and for the other the starting point of their pilgrimage.

With the Portuguese expansion to India, Sagres Point was suddenly no longer seen as the end but rather the beginning of a new world. Animal owners also believe that this is a truly hallowed spot, and some even bury their deceased pets on the headland. It's quite a walk to the pet cemetery at the end of the world. The path follows the first stage of the Rota Vicentina long-distance hiking route, from the lighthouse on the point towards Vila do Bispo. You then take the route marked blue, that forks off from the main track towards the west and the sea, following the path along the clifftops with their breathtaking views and right through the Costa Vicentina nature reserve with its unspoilt flora.

The hiking trail leads right past the cemetery – you'll immediately recognise the pet graves with their piles of stones and photos of dogs and cats. From here you can get back on to the blue-green main route towards Vila do Bispo or walk back in the opposite direction to the lighthouse.

Address Rota Vicentina, Trilho dos Pescadores, stage 1 | **Getting there** A 22, exit 1 Lagos, N 125 to Sagres, turn right at the roundabout towards Farol and park at the lighthouse. Be sure to take enough drinking water with you | **Tip** You can visit the lighthouse on Cabo de São Vicente on Wednesdays between 2pm and 5pm. Wait in front of the brown door in the yard. Next to the café is a sculpture of St Vincent, who gave the cape its name.

SÃO BARTOLOMEU DE MESSINES

99_ The Archaeological Trail
Past red standing stones into the present

This hiking trail looks very enticing. It begins at a wooden notice next to the former village school in Vale Fuzeiros near São Bartolomeu de Messines. The route will lead you gently up and down through hilly Mediterranean pastures. Nature seems to spring to life overnight at the end of January, the rays of the sun warm the skin and the soul, mimosas blossom egg-yolk yellow, medlars creamy white and almond trees a delicate pink. Lavender and rosemary fill the air with their tangy sweet scents, clover blossoms stand out bright yellow in meadows of wild flowers. Occasionally you come across sheep and goats, with shepherds and dogs. A warm greeting of 'Bom dia!' ensures a friendly smile. On you go through the countryside. Sometimes you'll see a roof from far off or hear a car drive past, but otherwise the only sounds are the wind and the birds singing.

After around two kilometres you will reach a prehistoric necropolis, with four menhirs standing over two metres tall, made of a type of rust-red calcareous sandstone. The so-called *grés de Silves* rock is very rare, and particularly striking with its vivid colour. The group of standing stones marks the summit of a hill and four graves of a family that lived here during the Stone Age. A few metres to the side there are some graves of various sizes. The depressions sculpted into the red stone probably served as grave pits for a mother and her child or they may have been used for sacrificial rites.

The journey through time continues on from the Stone Age into the 3rd century A.D., and a necropolis from late antiquity with grave troughs and stone slabs. At the end of the seven-kilometre hiking route you reach the most recent archaeological excavation site: an old, disused cemetery. With the arrival of the Romans, most of the settlers from this valley moved away to live in Silves, the oldest city in the Algarve.

Address Circuito Arqueológico da Vilarinha, Escola Primária, Rua de Vale Fuzeiros, 8375 São Bartolomeu de Messines | **Getting there** A 22, exit 6, towards Silves, after the tunnel turn left over the bridge, right at the traffic lights, towards S. B. de Messines, turn left at the signpost for Circuito Arqueológico | **Tip** The two dams of Barragem do Funcho and Barragem do Arade are not far from here and can be reached on foot or by car.

SÃO BRÁS DE ALPORTEL

100__ The Cork Factory
How the cork gets from the tree into the bottle

According to the cork factory Novacortiça, a company in São Brás de Alportel that specialises in champagne corks, this land, in the foothills of the Serra do Calderāio, is where the best cork in the world is grown. The knowledge of how to produce cork stoppers, above all wine corks, is not new. In fact, cork has been one of Portugal's top export goods for over 2,000 years, and the gnarly 'parasol trees', known as *sobreiros*, have been cultivated for the cork industry in Portugal for just as long. The cork oak is particularly at home in southern Alentejo and on the Algarve, where it is dry and warm for months on end. While the main trunk of the tree stores water, the spongy layer of cork between the trunk and outer bark remains flexible and can be removed between May and August.

Despite the numerous patented processing methods and technological developments for the manufacture of a variety of products, cork is still harvested, as it always has been, by hand, one tree at a time, and only every 10 years – that's how long the cork needs to grow back. The semicircular pieces of bark, separated from the trunk with a short-handled axe and bare hands, are called *pranchas* and they serve as the basis for a huge range of items.

Cork is an ecologically valuable material with many uses in the building trade, and it is exported as far as Australia. It is also worked into exclusive fashion accessories, from handbags to umbrellas. The cork oak forest owners in Portugal are doing well, in fact business is booming. All around the world more and more people are using cork items in their everyday lives, in decoration or as jewellery. On a guided tour of the Novacortiça factory, visitors can find out how champagne corks are produced, so that, thanks to Portuguese skill and know-how, the bottle pops open gently and fine sparkling French champagne bubbles and foams out.

Address Novacortiça, Parque Industrial da Barracha, 8150 São Brás de Alportel, www.novacortica.pt | **Getting there** A 22, exit 14, towards São Brás de Alportel, then towards Tavira to Barracha; the factory is on the main road | **Tip** The Museu de Traje in São Brás is a museum of costume which also has displays on traditional life, old vehicles and an exhibition showing how cork used to be processed. If you want to find out more about cork oaks, walk the PR 2 SBA hiking route or follow the Rota Cortiça.

SILVES

101 The Library Cellar
Roman waste management

Silves is an archaeological treasure trove. In the urban areas alone there are over 200 sites with evidence of Roman and Moorish activity, and some date even further back to the seafaring Phoenicians. They all tell the story of how the former capital of the Algarve grew up on the banks of the Arade, 18 kilometres upriver from the sea. At the beginning there was the fortress, or rather watchtower, from which the course of the river Arade can be observed all the way down to the modern water tower in Portimão. From there the view extends to the mouth of the Arade and the Catarina fort. In this way the guards in the three watch posts could communicate with each other within seconds, using smoke or mirror signals.

Initially, the citizens of Silves all lived inside the citadel on the crest of the hill, protected behind a thick rampart several metres high. From there the city expanded downhill towards the river and to this day it is enclosed by three ramparts with 16 watchtowers. Just like in any other stronghold, protection, defence and a supply of drinking water must be ensured. Without drinking water, even the best ramparts and the best weapons are useless. In Silves, two underground cisterns provided sufficient drinking water, and even the castle's own reservoir contained enough for a whole year. No wonder that Silves was able to hold out until the very end of the *Reconquista*.

At least as important as fresh water is a functioning system for sewage and waste disposal. The Romans recognised this and created a system of canals down from the castle into the river. Waste was separated and either burnt or composted. Back then the street cleaners lived right next to their place of work in their own quarter. This area was uncovered during the construction of the new public library in Silves and preserved; it is now visible behind protective glass in the cellar.

Address Biblioteca Municipal, Rua Latino Coelho 1, 8300 Silves | **Getting there** A 22, exit 7, towards Silves, after the tunnel go left over the bridge, then right, at the next turn-off left, then left again at the self-service shop; park at Praça Al-Mu'tamid | **Hours** Mon – Fri 9.30am – 6.30pm | **Tip** On the Al-Mu'tamid square there is street art by Bamby as well as fountains, Arabian princes in marble and Arabian poetry engraved on large tablets. Past the library the road leads uphill, via an ancient flight of steps, to the castle and Café Inglés, where there is live music at weekends.

SILVES

102 The Cross of Portugal
Manueline masterpiece with history

Portugal is famous for its Manueline sculpture, a nationally distinctive style of architectural ornamentation that put Portuguese art on the map in the reign of Dom Manuel I. The king left himself a lasting memorial in this style when he instructed the building of the Jerónimos Monastery in Lisbon. Stone mooring ropes, twisted into huge knots, embellish church doorways, high altars and cross vaults. Elaborately carved human faces, enchanting blossom, exotic animals, archangels, apostles and local matadors began to decorate the churches, monasteries and chapels of Portugal in the early 16th century. Some works are better known than others due to their particularly striking artistic dexterity – for example, the Cross of Portugal in Silves.

It stands almost three metres tall, majestically displayed in a pavilion next to the courthouse. The weathered sandstone appears crumbly, the artwork fragile, almost as if a gust of wind could blow it away. On one side you can make out Jesus on the cross, his face delicately modelled, contorted in dismay, the mouth open in a stifled cry. On the other side the Blessed Virgin Mary holds her dead son in her arms. A masterpiece of Manueline craftsmanship, but not strictly original – this is in fact a variant of other designs.

The front and back faces of the Cross of Portugal are taken from famous models. The same motifs are on an original cross in the vestry of the parish church of Ferragudo. It graced the altar in the Rosário chapel, on the rocky outcrop of the same name on the Arade river, which was sadly completely destroyed by the earthquake in 1755. This is where the victorious Crusaders under the king Dom Afonso III gave thanks to Our Lady of the Rosary for the capture of the Moorish royal city of Silves. The magnificent two-sided cross, based on the old icon, was commissioned for Silves in memory of this battle.

Address Cruz de Portugal, Roundabout N 124, 8300 Silves | **Getting there** A 22, exit 6, towards Silves, after the tunnel go left over the bridge, then right at the traffic lights, to the roundabout by the courthouse; park there | **Tip** Near the Cross of Portugal there are some metal sculptures by Carlos de Oliveira Correia. At the roundabout is a cork farmer with his donkey, and seated female factory workers punching out wine corks.

SILVES

103 The New City Hall
A reckless three-way liaison

The sensual frisson of the reckless liaison between the 11th-century poet-king of Seville, Al-Mu'tamid, and his grand vizier in Silves, Ibn' Ammar, is a source of inspiration to this day; countless lyrical aphorisms have been dedicated to their fatal affair. Ibn' Ammar was a penniless poet-adventurer before his rise to power at the court. The king's wife elbowed her way in between Al-Mu'tamid and his beloved – she didn't want to share her husband with anyone else, least of all a man. Al-Mu'tamid was the ruler of the biggest caliphate of all time, but he was possessed by love for his wife and at the same time driven by desire for his grand vizier. His torn heart made him an ambivalent ruler, and he began spending more and more time in his veranda palace in Silves, rather than in Seville, writing passionate love letters to his favourite wife and erotic messages to his lover.

One day Al-Mu'tamid's wife had had enough of this love triangle, so she devised a cunning trick to displace her rival. Her plan worked, but only in part. Al-Mu'tamid did distance himself from his lover after the spiteful scenes of jealousy his wife contrived. Ibn'Ammar however did not back off in his turn, but instead betrayed his king to the Crusaders. Sentenced to death for this act, Ibn' Ammar did not have to wait long for his execution. None other than Al-Mu'tamid himself put his former friend and lover to death. But too late – Silves fell. Al-Mu'tamid was imprisoned, the caliphate ended, and he never saw his wife again.

Today it is the city council that governs in Silves' new city hall, but Al-Mu'tamid remains omnipresent, and you almost feel that you can hear him whispering in the neo-Moorish atrium, confessing his desire for his lover just before he puts the knife to his throat with the words, 'Don't forget that I was the one who made your hidden flower blossom.'

Address Paço de Concelho, Largo do Município, 8300 Silves | **Getting there** A 22, exit 7, towards Silves, then towards S. B. de Messines, turn left at the self-service shop and follow the main road to the square at the city hall | **Hours** Mon–Fri 9am–5pm | **Tip** Just down from the city hall, under the arcades, is the old *pastelaria* Café da Rosa; on the square nearby is the ancient Pelourinho pillory.

TAVIRA

104 The House of Álvaro de Campos
The author that never existed

'I've already said that I don't want anything. Don't come to me with conclusions! Death is the only conclusion.' A remarkably morbid perting shot from an author from Tavira named Álvaro de Campos. He was born on a farm, where the horizon began on the beach beyond the veranda and the donkey walked in circles around the well, marking out the world and its magnitude. After studying to be a shipbuilding engineer in Glasgow, Campos returned to Portugal and settled in Lisbon, but did not take up a career, determined instead to devote himself to the art of writing.

His works are distinguished by an almost infantile simplicity. He repeatedly extols his childhood, and the aunts who rocked him to sleep on their laps with their gentle singing. Campos' poems are shaped by the urban milieu of Tavira at the turn of the 20th century. Fernando Pessoa described his 'fellow poet' from the Algarve as tall and gaunt, with a slightly hunched gait.

Remarkable words about an author who never existed, but rather, together with three other fictional alter egos – or heteronyms, as he termed them – came from the pen of the poet and author Fernando Pessoa. Campos served Pessoa as a channel for his own naive style of poetry that he otherwise kept secret, but could explore without fear behind the mask of the melancholic figure he created.

It was a brilliant literary coup. Through Campos, Pessoa was able to express his desires without revealing himself. In Tavira, the literary estate of a certain Jara funded the city library, and Pessoa's heteronym later gave it its name. A poetic homage to a fictional author, the Álvaro de Campos house in Tavira remembers Fernando Pessoa and his alter ego with literary salons, poetic trails and exhibitions.

Address Casa Álvaro de Campos, Rua da Galeria 9, 8800 Tavira | **Getting there** A22, exit 16, towards Tavira, park at the Franciscan church, walk towards Centro and through the old city gate at the main square into Rua da Galeria | **Tip** Continuing uphill, you will reach the Santa Maria quarter with its fortified castle, lookout tower and church. On the way is the Palácio da Galeria museum, where you can see from the inside one of Tavira's celebrated hipped roofs, which are found nowhere else in Portugal.

TAVIRA

105 __ Quatro Aguas
Where four waterways meet

Having just passed through a residential area, the road now suddenly leads through the salt marshes before the gates of the city of Tavira. As far as the eye can see, on either side of the road, brine glistens in the sun in basins large and small and dazzling mountains of salt are reflected in the seawater of the fish-breeding ponds. From May to September you can walk through the salt marshes on foot or watch the salt harvest or the mussel farmers at work from your car. If you ask politely, they'll probably invite you to come closer, and then they'll be happy to show you their secrets – how they look for lugworms, pull razor clams from the sand, remove mussels from the rocks and find cockles buried in the sand.

The road ends in Quatro Aguas by the harbour. The harbour jetty is a dead end; the only way on from here is by boat. There are four directions: upriver, to the west, to the east or towards the sea. For this reason, the area has been called Quatro Aguas from time immemorial. Here the Rio Gilão merges with its tributaries in the lagoon between the islands of Ilha de Tavira and Ilha Cabanas de Tavira, and washes into the sea between the waves. From a bird's-eye perspective, this place looks like a waterway junction. The upstream peninsula, with forked tideways and marshland, is still a pristine stretch of Algarve coast, where you can buy seafood freshly harvested as it always has been.

From here you can continue on with the ferry to the islands off the coast of Tavira, and go for long walks along the beaches, with nothing in sight but sand, sky and the horizon. In the evening all is quiet around the jetty, as the setting sun drenches the dunes in fiery colours. Inland, Tavira rises up with its unique hipped-roof cityscape, crowned by the former knights' castle and dotted with 21 church towers and cupolas. It's simply magical.

Address Cais das Quatro Aguas, 8800 Tavira | **Getting there** A 22, exit 16, towards Tavira, towards the Estação CP train station, follow the main road, turn right before the bridge on to the Estrada to Quatro Aguas | **Tip** Santa Luzia, the Algarve's octopus capital, lies to the west. Here you can feast on the cephalopods prepared in hundreds of deliciously different ways. Beyond Santa Luzia is a sluice, from where a miniature railway will take you down to the beach of Praia de Barril, known for its Anchor Graveyard.

TAVIRA

106   The Tuna Fish Museum
The bull of the sea

Tavira and tuna fish are connected through 2,000 years of fishing culture. The shallow water in the lagoons along the coast near Tavira were once one of the spawning grounds of the powerful fish, silvery-blue and shining, with large eyes and delicious dark red flesh. In order to hunt and overpower large numbers of these 100-kilogram-weight giants of the ocean with the fishing equipment available to them at the time, the local fishing community used to set up special traps called *armaçoes de atum*. The tuna fish swam into these labyrinthine bottom-set nets as if into a kind of tunnel, but then couldn't find their way out. Tricked by the fisherman, they could then be corralled, surrounded and killed with spears.

When cornered and threatened like this, the fish would attack the fishermen and fight for their lives. The tuna thus earned the nickname *touro do mar*, or 'bull of the sea'. Its meaty flesh is also dark red, like that of a bull. The back fillet was particularly in demand among innkeepers – cunning cooks could serve up the fillet, with lots of seasoning, as expensive beef. Cut into wafer-thin slices, the air-dried 'sea ham' *muxama* is a particular delicacy, and it's even more in demand for its roe. Garum paste made from tuna fish liver was a highly concentrated, spicy fish sauce that was all the rage in the budding gourmet cuisine of Imperial Rome. Hearty fish stews were made using the oily belly meat.

Right up into the 1970s the traditional tuna fishing of Tavira was one of the main sources of income for the local community, until one day, after hundreds of years of persistent overfishing, not a single tuna fish was tempted into the fishermen's traps. Hotel Vila Galé is on the site where the tuna fishing community formerly lived. It has a small museum, with displays documenting how tuna fishing off the coast of Tavira used to work.

Address Hotel Vila Galé Albacora, Quatro Águas, 8800 Tavira, www.vilagale.com | **Getting there** A 22, exit 16, towards Vila Real Santo António, go on to the Gran Plaza shopping centre and from there follow the sign on the roundabout to the hotel, three kilometres through the Tavira marshland | **Hours** Daily 8am – 7pm (closed in winter) | **Tip** The ruins of the Forte do Rato are within sight of the hotel.

TUNES

107 — The Railway Station
A rebellious bank robber and his greatest coup

The Celtiberians were already considered decidedly headstrong at the time when the Roman military leader Marcus Aurelius was occupying the country west of the Guadiana river. During the subsequent Moorish rule, the Algarvians adjusted to the Islamic way of life, but kept mainly to themselves. In the Middle Ages, Spain tried to reconquer what was the county of Portucale several times; they also failed in the face of Lusitanian stubbornness, just as Napoleon Bonaparte did centuries later.

In fascist Portugal in the last century, there were men like Hermínio da Palma Inácio, son of a level-crossing attendant from Tunes, who rebelled against the regime. He joined the underground and took part in militant activities from the very beginning. During the unsuccessful attempted coup against Salazar in 1947, the PIDE secret police arrested Palma Inácio for sabotaging military aircraft. A short time later he hijacked a plane belonging to the Portuguese airline TAP on its flight from Casablanca to Lisbon – incidentally, the only politically motivated hijack of an aeroplane in Portugal to date – and forced the pilots to fly low over Lisbon in order to drop pamphlets with antifascist slogans on to the streets. Afterwards Palma Inácio founded the notorious activist movement Liga de Unidade e Acção Revolucionária, or LUAR, whose members later played a decisive role in the Carnation Revolution.

In July 1967 Palma Inácio pulled off his greatest coup. Together with his comrades he robbed the Portuguese national bank in Figueira da Foz, making off to France with 30 million escudos, the equivalent of around seven million euros, in a small plane. The railway worker's house that was his family home has long since been demolished – in its place is now Tunes station. A biography recently published in Portugal tells the story of Palma Inácio and the 50 years he spent in exile.

Address Tunes Station, Rua do Armazém 12, 8365 Tunes | **Getting there** A 22, exit 9, on the motorway IC 1 towards Lisbon, exit Tunes, follow signs to Estação | **Tip** Tunes is a junction station for the Algarve and Algarve–Lisbon routes. From here the Alfa Pendular express train reaches Lisbon in a little over two hours.

VILA DO BISPO

108 Praia do Castelejo
An informer's last step

Praia do Castelejo is definitely one of the most fascinating beach bays on the west coast, especially here at Torre de Aspa, where the slate-grey cliffs tower 135 metres out of the sea. The sandy bay feels a galaxy away from the typical tourist's Algarve and is visited only by those in the know – surfers, naked swimmers and people who just want to turn off. You won't get any internet reception here, nor even a telephone signal.

The access road leads from Vila do Bispo through the Costa Vicentina nature reserve to the beach. Halfway there on the left is a picnic area, where the circular hiking trail Trilho Ambiental do Castelejo VBP PR 1 begins, leading through a stone pine forest to the Torre de Aspa cliffs. The former watch post sits alone on the cliffs between heaven and earth. It immediately brings to mind Agatha Christie's whodunit *Why Didn't They Ask Evans?* – and as it happens, this place really does have a murder-mystery story to tell.

During World War II, a lighthouse keeper here is said to have spied on Allied scout aircraft for the then German consul. He would contact the consul by radio, and he in turn would warn the pilots of the German Luftwaffe when to avoid the airspace over Sagres. The German consul's spy later became a paid informer, earning considerable baksheesh from the PIDE secret police. The rumour spread that he was spying on his neighbours, and would snitch to the militia if they spoke out against the regime. One night the local community is said to have come together and ambushed the spy, forcing him over the edge of the cliff at Torre de Aspa. He didn't fall immediately, but at some point he disappeared.

The outcrop on the cliff, according to local lore, is the spy still trying to climb back up the rock. It's actually not hard to see this shape as a climber – in fact you might even wonder why he isn't moving.

Address Torre de Aspa, Praia do Castelejo, 8650 Vila do Bispo | **Getting there** A 22, exit 1, towards Sagres, exit Vila do Bispo, towards Mercado, drive past and turn right at the junction to Praia de Castelejo | **Tip** Just after the picnic area, a road and dirt track forks off to the right to the Miradouro de Castelejo viewpoint, from where you can enjoy views of two sandy bays, the watch house, Torre de Aspa and the outcrop.

VILA NOVA DE CACELA

109 — Cabanas Square

A revolutionary discovers art as a haven of peace

Manuel dos Santos Cabanas was a former Grand Master of the oldest Freemasonry lodge in Portugal, the Grande Oriente Lusitano. The son of smallholders from Vila Nova de Cacela, in the district of Vila Real de Santo António, he was already fighting the nascent dictatorship in Portugal as a young man. Cabanas was arrested for the first time when he tried to steal food for people in need from a military barracks, but that didn't stop him rebelling, through both words and actions, against the social inequalities that prevailed during the dictatorship. His offences were always serious enough for him to be taken into custody for a few days, but not to be locked away for good.

In search of like-minded people, Cabanas moved to Lisbon and rallied a revolutionary group around himself with the aim of mobilising the underground, agitating public opinion against the regime and recruiting new activists. To this end he used democratic slogans, took part in literary discussions in the Bertrand bookshop and in political debates in various bars and cafés. One day he discovered a passion for the art of wood engraving, and he went on to create a large body of work over the course of the years. He became a member of the National Society of Fine Arts, and won the trust of his fellow masons as the Grand Master of the lodge.

The co-founder of the Socialist Party saw himself as having finally reached the zenith of his political work in 1973, when he was appointed a member of parliament by the founding father of the democracy, Mário Soares. A bust in memory of the former Freemasonry Grand Master, politician and artist Cabanas, unveiled personally by Mário Soares, can be found on Largo de Manuel Cabanas in Vila Nova de Cacela. A collection of Cabanas' wood engravings – the only one in the whole of Portugal – is on display in the Vila Real de Santo António city archive.

Address Largo Manuel Cabanas 10, 8900 Vila Nova de Cacela | **Getting there** A 22, exit 17, towards Tavira, in Vila Nova de Cacela follow the signs to Junta de Freguesia (town hall) | **Tip** In Santa Rita, north-west of Cacela Nova, is the Stone Age megalithic tomb of Túmulo Megalítico de Santa Rita.

VILA REAL DE SANTO ANTÓNIO

110_ The Dune Sanctuary
Encountering chameleons in the wild

Stand clear of the doors. An evocative cage lift takes you up to the lantern at the top of the Vila Real de Santo António lighthouse. The lighthouse marks the south-eastern cardinal point of Portugal and watches over shipping at the entrance to the boundary river Rio Guadiana. A set of ladders and a door painted red are now all that separate the visitor from the platform that encircles the entire tower above the tops of massive pine trees, at a dizzying height of 50 metres.

The pine forest in Vila Real de Santo António rolls out like a dark green carpet all the way along the beach to Monte Gordo, taking its place in the prospect between the sky and the sea. A shady realm populated by insects, rodents and birds on the fluid border between Portugal and Spain, it's a local recreation area with fitness routes for cycling, jogging and walking. The forest offers protection from the scorching heat that summer brings between June and September. In the year 2000, the forest was declared a conservation area, the Mata Nacional das Dunas Litorais de VRSA. Since then it has provided a legally protected habitat for chameleons.

Hardly bigger than a saucer, the common chameleon would fit on the palm of your hand. Their front feet are like hands, with five tiny round suction cups. This gives the reptile fantastic grip for climbing. Its skin is soft, warm and smooth. The little lizard moves ponderously through the branches as if in slow motion, poised between pine needles and pine cones, motionlessly observing its surroundings, until an insect catches its attention and it devours it in a split second, using its lightning-fast tongue that rolls out and in again in a flash. Of course, you can't see these mini-dinosaurs from the lighthouse – you'll have to walk into the forest for that, ideally armed with lots of time, patience and a pair of binoculars.

Address Mata Nacional das Dunas Litorais, Vila Real de Santo António 393, 8900 Vila Real de Santo António | **Getting there** A 22, exit 18, towards Vila Real de Santo António and Monte Gordo, turn right at the first roundabout after the Lidl supermarket and park; start from the picnic area | **Tip** You can walk through the forest from the mouth of the Guadiana to the beach resort of Monte Gordo. On the way there are picnic areas, a playground and a freshwater lagoon near Aldeia Nova, which is a particularly good place to watch chameleons.

VILA REAL DE SANTO ANTÓNIO

111 — The Ferry to Portugal
The end of the journey is the start of the journey

Those who wish to travel to Portugal in style go by boat. More specifically, they take the ferry from Spain over the river that forms the border, Rio Guadiana. It's no longer the only way, since the bridge of Ponte do Guadiana now connects the two countries, but the ferry crossing is fun, and it will get you into the swing of the Algarve and the inherent nonchalance of its inhabitants.

The region's lifeline flows between the banks of the border cities of Ayamonte in Spain and Vila Real de Santo António in Portugal towards the Atlantic Ocean. During the passage, the Algarve will already surprise you with its indescribably translucent clear light and powerful colours. Everything about the Algarve glows with vivid intensity – the sky, sea, sand, houses, trees and castles.

The first thing you see is the fort of Castro Marim, and only then does the beautiful new city of Vila Real de Santo António emerge on the Portuguese side of the river. The rest of the Algarve proves just as contrasting as these two places, always revealing something new and different. With the spirited clatter of espresso cups, the rolling 'r' and the *buenas* of the Spanish language still in your ears, your curiosity about the way of life and language that awaits on the other side of the river grows. The bow of the ferry or the top deck next to the bridge are the best places to stand and watch Ayamonte growing smaller and Vila Real de Santo António getting bigger. There is little traffic on the promenade along the river, the boats in the harbour seem to sparkle. The promenade welcomes fresh arrivals with a maritime nonchalance, with street art and café culture, with understated elegance and a huge portion of *joie de vivre*.

You are welcomed with a 'Bem vindo no Algarve', and in that moment it doesn't matter whether you are arriving for the first time or coming back – let the journey begin.

Address Travessia Guadiana, Porto de Recreio do Guadiana, Avenida da República, 8900 Vila Real de Santo António | **Getting there** A 22, exit 18, to Vila Real de Santo António and Porto (harbour) | **Tip** The recently refurbished Grand Hotel Guadiana is a romantic renaissance flagship for the whole city. A wander to the main square of Marquês de Pombal takes you through the youngest city on the Algarve, with its Pombaline architecture.

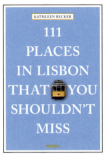

Kathleen Becker
**111 Places in Lisbon
That You Shouldn't Miss**
ISBN 978-3-7408-0383-4

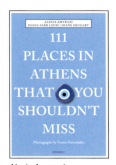

Alexia Amvrazi,
Diana Farr Louis, Diane Shugart
**111 Places in Athens
That You Shouldn't Miss**
ISBN 978-3-7408-0377-3

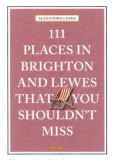

Alexandra Loske
**111 Places in Brighton and
Lewes That You Shouldn't Miss**
ISBN 978-3-7408-0255-4

Fabrizio Ardito
**111 Places in Malta
That You Shouldn't Miss**
ISBN 978-3-7408-0261-5

Benjamin Haas,
Leonie Friedrich
**111 Places in Buenos Aires
That You Must Not Miss**
ISBN 978-3-7408-0260-8

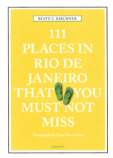

Beate C. Kirchner
**111 Places in Rio de Janeiro
That You Must Not Miss**
ISBN 978-3-7408-0262-2

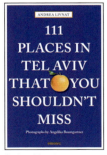

Andrea Livnat,
Angelika Baumgartner
**111 Places in Tel Aviv
That You Shouldn't Miss**
ISBN 978-3-7408-0263-9

Kai Oidtmann
**111 Places in Iceland
That You Shouldn't Miss**
ISBN 978-3-7408-0030-7

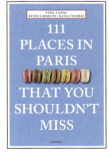

Sybil Canac,
Renée Grimaud, Katia Thomas
**111 Places in Paris
That You Shouldn't Miss**
ISBN 978-3-7408-0159-5

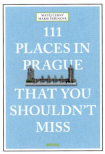

Matěj Černý, Marie Peřinová
111 Places in Prague That You Shouldn't Miss
ISBN 978-3-7408-0144-1

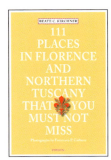

Beate C. Kirchner
111 Places in Florence and Northern Tuscany That You Must Not Miss
ISBN 978-3-95451-613-1

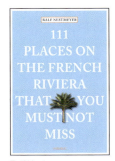

Ralf Nestmeyer
111 Places on the French Riviera That You Must Not Miss
ISBN 978-3-95451-612-4

Giulia Castelli Gattinara, Mario Verin
111 Places in Milan That You Must Not Miss
ISBN 978-3-95451-331-4

Petra Sophia Zimmermann
111 Places in Verona and Lake Garda That You Must Not Miss
ISBN 978-3-95451-611-7

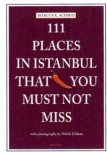

Marcus X. Schmid
111 Places in Istanbul That You Must Not Miss
ISBN 978-3-95451-423-6

Annett Klingner
111 Places in Rome That You Must Not Miss
ISBN 978-3-95451-469-4

Ralf Nestmeyer
111 Places in Provence That You Must Not Miss
ISBN 978-3-95451-422-9

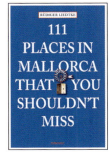

Rüdiger Liedtke
111 Places on Mallorca That You Shouldn't Miss
ISBN 978-3-95451-281-2

Bibliography and sources

Amadao, Adeleide: *A Carta de foral da Vila de Albufeira e seu tempo: D. Manuel I. 1504*. Edição Câmara Municipal de Albufeira 1993

Azevedo, Carlos & Brummel, Chester: *Igrejas de Portugal*. Lisboa, Venda Nova Bertrand, D.L. 1985

Borges, Victor: *Apokalypsis*. Arandis Editora 2012

Costa Vieira, Carla: *O levantamento contra as tropas francesas*. Olhão Junho 1808. Edição município de Olhão 2009

Coutinho, Valdemar: *Algarve Cercos, Fortes e Castellos*. Algarve em foco 1999

Freitas Eduardo de e Matias Ferreira, Vítor: *A Serra de Caldeirão*. Roteiro Sócio cultural. Faro IN LOCO 1999

Gonçalves, Ilena Luís Candeias: *Escritores Portugueses do Algarve*. Edições Colibri 2000

Guedes, Rui Gonçalves & Veríssimo Serrão, D. Joaquim: *Tavira História Viva*. Edição Câmara

João, Mariano & Sacadeira, João Paulo Aljezur: *O Coração da Costa Vicentina*. Edição bilingue. Edição Municipio de Aljezur 2016

Martins, José António: *Monografia de Lagos*. Estúdio histórico da Freguesia de S. Sebastião de Lagos 1989

Martins, José António: *Aljezur e os descobrimentos portugueses*. Junta de Freguesia de Aljezur 2016

Mendes Pinto, María Helena & Mendes Pinto, Victor: *As Misericórdias do Algarve*. Ministério de Saúde e Direcção geral de assistençia 1968

Oliveira Xavier Ataide de: *Estômbar*. Typografia Universal, Porto 1987

Oliveira, Xavier Ataide de: *Monografia do Concelho de Vila Real de Santo António*. Algarve em foco 1989

Paula, Rui M.: *Faro. Evolução Urbana e Património*. Edição Câmara Municipal de Faro 1993

Paula, Rui M.: *Ossonoba – Santa Maria – Ibn Harun – Faro*. Edição Câmara Municipal de Faro 2014

Pereira, Pedro & Campos Inácio, Nuno: *Carbonário e outros Revolucionários*. Arandis Editora 2014

Pinto da Silva, João Belmiro & Paços de Ferreira: *Benafim - Memorias e Identidade*. Héstia Editores 2006

Raposo, Isabel: *Na roda do Tempo*. Casa do Povo Alte 1995, Municipal de Tavira 2001

Vairinhos Malobba, Patrícia Mimoso: *Estoi. Identidade e transformação*. Edição Câmara Municipal de Faro 2009

Acknowledgements

First and foremost I would like to thank the staff at the Biblioteca Municipal Manuel Teixeira Gomes in Portimão, who were always there with helpful advice and a real feel for the right literature to help me in my work on this book. I thank my husband Arménio for having the patience of a saint when I was in the final stages of writing this book, during which I was maniacally attached to my desk. I would like to thank my colleague Kerstin Lange for bringing Emons' 111 Places series to my attention. Thank you very much to Berenike Jacob for everything that she didn't say. Nuno Campos Inácio from Arandis-Editora, a cultural publishing imprint in the Algarve, was a great help to me on several tricky sources. Muito Obrigada, Nuno! I would like to give special thanks to Katharina Theml for her valuable and constructive collaboration in the editing phase. Thank you also to Sonja Erdmann for the second run-through and the whole of the Emons team for their support from A to Z in the realisation of this wonderful project as well as Laura Olk, Gillian Tait and Tom Ashforth for their work on the translation of the english edition. The final thank you goes to my readers who accompany me through this book and to 111 places along the Algarve.

The author

Catrin George Ponciano, born in Bielefeld in 1967, has lived since 1999 in the Algarve in her adoptive home of Portugal, where she works as an author and tour guide. She regularly publishes photo reportages about Portugal, writes travel books and accompanies tour groups through Portugal from North to South and vice versa. www.catringeorge.com